D0600736

GRILLS & GREENS

OTHER BOOKS BY LINDA ZIMMERMAN

ㄋ ɪɪɪɪ ㄷ

Puddings, Custards and Flans

*Cobblers, Crumbles and Crisps
and Other Old-Fashioned Fruit Desserts*
(with Peggy Mellody)

GRILLS & GREENS

Easy Recipes for Salads and Sandwiches

LINDA ZIMMERMAN & GERRI GILLILAND

Photographs by Ann Mitchell   Tabletop Styling by Robin Tucker
Food Styling by Linda Zimmerman

CLARKSON POTTER / PUBLISHER
NEW YORK

Copyright © 1993 by Linda Zimmerman and Gerri Gilliland
Photographs copyright © 1993 by Ann Mitchell

All rights reserved. No part of this book may be reproduced or transmitted
in any form or by any means, electronic or mechanical, including
photocopying, recording, or by any information storage and retrieval system,
without permission in writing from the publisher.

Published by Clarkson N. Potter, Inc., 201 East 50th Street, New York, New York, 10022.
Member of the Crown Publishing Group.

Random House, Inc. New York, Toronto, London, Sydney, Auckland

CLARKSON N. POTTER, POTTER, and colophon are trademarks of Clarkson N. Potter, Inc.

Manufactured in the United States of America

Design by Margaret Hinders

Library of Congress Cataloging-in-Publication Data

Zimmerman, Linda.
Grills & greens : recipes for salads and sandwiches/
Linda Zimmerman & Gerri Gilliland; photographs by Ann Mitchell;
tabletop styling by Robin Tucker; food styling by Linda Zimmerman.
1st ed.
Includes index.
1. Barbecue cookery. 2. Salads. 3. Sandwiches.
I. Gilliland, Gerri. II. Title. III. Title: Grills and greens.
TX840.B3Z56   1993
641.7′7—dc20   92-41129
CIP

ISBN 0-517-58589-8

1   3   5   7   9   10   8   6   4   2

First Edition

For Michael Maron—a good eater, a good listener, a best friend

Linda Zimmerman

For my husband, Theodore Lonsway

Gerri Gilliland

ACKNOWLEDGMENTS

Book writing is not always a singular endeavor. Many personal and professional friends may participate throughout the process by sharing their expertise or just lending an encouraging ear. Special thanks are due to those who contributed their invaluable assistance during the writing of this book:

Rich Axelrod of The Ultimate Edge kept our knives very, very sharp. Mary Bragg, who now lives in Cabo San Lucas, gave us the terrific Valentina Indoor Grill that we wore out. Linda Burum, who is always right, provided insightful editorial comment. Peggy Mellody and Mary Stec both spent time and energy testing recipes in a pinch. Both Helen Bercovitz and Rochelle Huppin's friendship and support made life delicious and uplifting.

Mimi Z. licked her little whiskers over every mixed grill, and Brigid appreciated every little taste.

There could never be a book without Barbara Lowenstein, who always proves to be as good a friend as an agent, and Shirley Wohl, who is the kind of editor every writer deserves.

Sheelagh O'Connor and the staff at Gilliland's were always cheerfully helpful, as were the guys in the kitchen (Isidoro Tapia, Estephan Garcia, Alfredo Garcia, Agustine Marcial, and Hector Martinez) who chopped, diced, and prepped on so many Saturday mornings.

Thank you to the following people who so generously provided knowledge and/or products while we tested the recipes and shot the photographs: Tracey Athanassiadis of Malibu Greens, The Beverly Hills Cheese Shop, Carole Borah, Cabot Creamery of Vermont, Gary Chorost of LA Eats, Tony DiLembo and Breadworks, DiMare Homestead Tomatoes, David George of Fresh Endeavors, Stephanie Johnson of J. R. Brooks & Son, Pam Lewis of BW Provisions, Beth Mahaffey of the Florida Tomato Committee, W. Allen Oliver, Jr., of J & R Manufacturing, Peacock Cheese, Stewart Rembert of Louisiana Seafood, Jill Sandin of Frieda, Inc., The Spice Hunter, John Waugh of Porcelain Metals Corporation, Laurie Wilson of the National Turkey Federation, and World Variety Produce.

Grilling and cooking equipment was donated by Evan Baker at Paykel in Santa Monica, Broilmaster, Burton Stove Top Grills, Chantry and Victor Kitchenware, Char Broil, Charcoal Companion, Cuisinart, Ducane Gas Grills, El Asador Stove-Top Grills, Frieling USA (hot rock), Griffo Grill and Mick Freeman, Hasty Bake Charcoal Ovens, Jackes-Evans Chimney Lighter, Kingsford™ Pro™ Charcoal Grill, Lanson Tools and Knives, Le Creuset, Maverick Grills, Maxim Indoor Barbecue, Pyramid Portable Outdoor Grilling Systems, Salday Products (Bar-B-Q Pizza Baker), Sun Beam, Tefal Smoke-Free Indoor Barbeque, Weber Grills, and Vitantonio.

Tesoro in Los Angeles provided the beautiful plates and accessories used in photographing the following dishes: Isidoro's Calcutta Chicken; Grilled Wild Mushrooms, Radicchio, and Sprouts Sandwich; Sausage and Polenta Sandwich with Dried and Fresh Tomato-Herb Relish; Skirt Steaks with Avocado-Stuffed Chiles; and Lula Bertran's Grilled Shrimp and Scallops with Mango Mayonnaise and Fried Cilantro.

Additional props were generously lent by Stephanie Puddy and Brian Toffoli.

Our location photography was an enjoyable experience because of Leslie Rosenstock, who provided her wonderful house; Brennen Ivie, who proved to be a tireless photo assistant; and food stylist Nona Baer, who graciously helped out on that busy day when we needed someone who knew all the tricks.

And lastly, thank you, thank you, thank you to stylist Robin Tucker, whose expertise, creativity, and patience are more appreciated than these few words can express, and to Ann Mitchell, whose sparkling talent is apparent in every onc of the beautiful photographs in this book.

CONTENTS

INTRODUCTION

The first meal of grills and greens most likely was enjoyed around a prehistoric campfire, when early man sat down with a chunk of fire-seared mastodon and a handful of wild dandelions.

Grilling—cooking over fire—is, without a doubt, the world's first definitive cooking method.

Greens, such as lettuces, cabbages, and herbs, also stand tall in gastronomical history. The ancient Egyptians cultivated lettuce, as did the Babylonians and Greeks. By the time of Imperial Rome, the *herba salata*—or salted greens—was a popular salad course that was dressed with herbs, oil, and vinegar and served either as a starter or at the end of the meal as a palate-cleansing digestive.

Perhaps grills and greens never appeared together on the same plate at a Roman banquet, but it's apparent that the everyday diet of the Mediterranean has heavily influenced our eating habits today.

Dining in the nineties has taken a major about-face since the not-so-long-ago days of haute cuisine and its cream, butter, and protein-heavy plates. Our sophisticated palates now require good flavor, but our health-conscious sensibilities demand the integration of a lower ratio of protein with a higher ratio of low-fat and carbohydrate ingredients (whole grains and fresh vegetables and fruits). We also want to be able to prepare meals in a minimum amount of time.

Whether grills are accompanied by lightly dressed composed salads of crisp greens mixed with seasonal produce, grains, or pastas, or made into hefty sandwiches, the combination of grills and greens is now being predominantly featured on tables all over the world. But this is also the kind of rustic fare that has been common throughout southern Europe for centuries. So, we've actually come full circle. The food is healthy, devoid of saturated fats, quick to fix, spectacular in presentation, and above all, delicious—truly the best kind of eating.

While not actually conceived with these thoughts in mind, the recipes in this book fit perfectly into today's life-style and take less than an hour to cook, with the majority cooking in under half an hour. Many of the recipes are scaled-down versions of dishes served at Gilliland's Cafe and Lula (Gerri's two restaurants). The rest are from various sources: our collaborative efforts (one of us would have the idea for the grill, the other for the greens, or vice versa); our individual kitchens and cooking classes; and, gratefully, good friends.

GRILLING BASICS

Grilling is a dry-heat method of quickly cooking food over fire or very hot coals (unless you live in England, where cooking under the fire in the stove—"broiling" in the United States—is called grilling and cooking over hot coals is called barbecuing). Whether done over coals or gas, or on an electric grill, direct-heat grilling sears the food and seals in the juices. This type of grilling is ideal for cooking small and tender cuts of meat, fish and seafood, poultry, and vegetables. All of the grilled food discussed in this book is cooked by direct heat.

TYPES OF GRILLS

Depending upon the type of grill you prefer, where you'll be cooking most often—indoors or out—and the amount of space you have, you'll find that there is a grill available to best suit your needs.

While any food cooked outdoors over hot burning coals or wood seems to taste best, the type of equipment used is a personal choice. If you have space for only a small stovetop or an electric grill that sits on the countertop, you might not achieve the identical "outdoor taste," but you'll achieve similar results. Just remember, a slight adjustment for the cooking times might be necessary, depending upon the equipment and other variables, such as the temperature of the food.

CHARCOAL GRILLS, which are probably the most common, come in various sizes. Whether you prefer a tiny, portable cast-iron Japanese hibachi for two, a square or rectangular covered cooker, or one of the beautiful round or oval covered kettles made of heavy-gauge steel with a baked-on porcelain enamel finish, you will achieve the same results with our recipes.

Hibachis, similar to open braziers, barbecue boxes—like the Hasty Bake—with hinged lids and adjustable fire boxes (also used for slow cooking and smoking), or kettles—like the Kingsford and Weber—all produce terrific results from cooking directly over charcoal or a combination of charcoal and aromatic woods.

Kettles, when used with their lids, work like convection ovens because of their top and bottom vents. Some even have easy-to-read thermometers built into the lids.

GAS GRILLS, which turn on and off just like gas ranges, have the advantage of not using messy charcoal. They're fueled by tanks of liquid propane (LP). Lava rocks sit above the gas jets and flavor the food almost as well as charcoal or wood briquettes. As the juices fall onto the lava rocks, flavor is released. Large chuck wagon–type grills, like the Weber, work with Flavorizer® Bars rather than rocks. They also have lids, so you can roast, slow barbecue, or smoke foods in them; some come with rotisseries.

ELECTRIC GRILLS for use indoors or outdoors are almost as popular as outdoor grills. They disassemble for easy cleaning and most cook virtually smoke-free. Timing will vary somewhat when using these grills. Keep in mind that the higher the wattage (1350 to 1650 watts), the more similar the performance to an outdoor grill. If the wattage is low (around 800 watts), the food will take longer to cook and scoring marks will be difficult to obtain. Some electric grills not only grill but can be used to steam, roast, and smoke.

STOVETOP GRILLS are used on top of gas, electric, or propane burners. Operating on the same principle as the tabletop grills used in Korean restaurants, stovetop grills sear and cook food fat-free on a smooth cooking surface. The grease drains away through drip slots into a porcelain-coated drip pan filled with water that sits atop the burner. Just as with some of the electric grills, the water in the drip pan eliminates smoke and splatter. Although the cooking surface has a nonstick coating, it's best to spray it with nonstick spray or to lightly oil after much use. These types of grills come in several round sizes as well as in a rectangular double-burner size that can easily grill a whole fish or enough food for six people.

PRESEASONED CAST-IRON GRILL PANS, like the Chantry Victor Grillpan or Le Creuset reversible grill, are also designed for stovetop grilling. The raised interior ridges have the same function as the rack of an outdoor grill. They score the food and sear in the flavor and juices. The melted fat falls into a gutter below, which runs around the perimeter of the pan and can easily be poured off after cooking. As with all cast iron, the pan must be preheated slowly and never scoured.

TYPES OF FUEL

Standard charcoal briquettes and hardwood lump charcoal, which is almost pure carbon, are easily started and burn hot, evenly, and clean. Hardwood lump charcoal, such as mesquite or oak, is oddly shaped chunks of charcoal that burn hotter and longer than standard briquettes. Olive wood briquettes, which are manufactured in Israel and add a subtle flavor, have just recently entered the market.

Light the coals about thirty minutes before starting to cook. They're ready to use when covered with a fine white ash.

Hardwood, noted as the original grilling fuel, does not burn as evenly as charcoal or hardwood charcoal and requires more time to become grill ready.

Aromatic wood chips (such as apple, alder, cherry, hickory, mesquite, oak, and pecan chips) are flavor enhancers, not fuel, and don't really do a whole lot unless they're used with a covered grill for longer cooking. For lighter flavor, they can be thrown right on the coals without first being soaked in water. As the chips slowly burn they impart a smoky essence to the food. Soaking chips in a flavored liquid such as wine, beer, or even fruit juice before adding them to the coals increases their intensity. Dried grape vine cuttings, basilwood, and dried fennel stalks also add a wonderful smoky flavor to meats, fish, and poultry when used either during cooking or just before the food is done.

LIGHTING THE FIRE

CHARCOAL STARTER FUEL is petroleum based. We don't recommend using it, since there are so many environment-saving alternatives that are easy to use and just as efficient.

If using starter fuel, don't add it to coals once the fire is established. Self-starting briquettes are presaturated with starter fuel. Never add them to already-lit coals.

CHIMNEY CHARCOAL LIGHTERS, although relatively new on the market, have actually been used in a homemade, crude state for years by campers and Boy Scouts. They're the best and fastest method for starting charcoal and they eliminate the need for chemical lighting fluids. Made of heavy galvanized metal, the lighter is shaped like a large coffee can, has air vents at the bottom and a wooden handle, and is divided horizontally by a heavy wire rack. The coals are piled on the interior rack, then a firestarter or crumpled newspaper placed underneath is lit. Working like a chimney, the air vents pull the hot flames up through the charcoal, which will be red-hot within fifteen minutes. The coals then can be easily poured into the grill.

FIRESTARTERS also eliminate the need for liquid chemical starters. Made of non-toxic compressed wood or corncobs that have been dipped in edible paraffin, they produce an intense and long-burning heat that easily ignites the coal. Two or three of them should be strategically placed among the coals, then lit. The coals will catch immediately and be ready in about thirty minutes.

ELECTRIC STARTERS are very easy to use. The starter is placed right in the coals, layered with more briquettes, then plugged in. After about ten minutes, when the coals have caught on, the starter should be removed, unplugged, and placed on a nonflammable surface to cool. The coals should be ready to use in twenty more minutes. The only disadvantage of an electric starter is that it requires either an outdoor outlet or a long extension cord so it can be plugged in.

ACCESSORIES AND TOOLS

HINGED GRILL BASKETS are placed on top of the grill. Instead of individually turning fish, burgers, vegetables, or any fragile, odd-shaped, or small pieces of food, the basket itself is turned, allowing the food to be perfectly cooked on both sides. They also prevent food from dropping into the coals. The one disadvantage of these baskets is that they make basting difficult.

STAINLESS OR PORCELAIN-COATED GRILLING RACKS also prevent delicate foods from falling into the coals. Depending on the brand, the surface is made either of close-worked metal mesh, like a window screen, or porcelain-covered, heavy-gauge steel with a multihole or grid pattern. The latter versions are stick resistant and easy to clean and have spatula-stop sides that simplify the removal of food. They're made to fit on top of any conventional round or rectangular gas or charcoal grill, as well as indoor range grills, like the Jenn-Air. Just recently, Griffo Grills introduced a porcelain-coated, grill-top wok. The bottom is perforated so the smoky flavor of the coals can permeate the food as you quickly stir-fry on top of the grill.

GAS GRILL SMOKING RACKS allow herbs and wood chips to be placed on a screen on top of the lava rocks for smoked flavor without dirtying or clogging the gas jets with ashes.

GRILLING TOOLS aimed at the consumer usually score high on looks and low on performance. They really can't do the job as well as heavy-duty professional tools. Look for the following at restaurant supply stores, where they are inexpensively priced, and gourmet cookware shops:

LONG-HANDLED, SPRING-LOADED, HEAVY-DUTY STAINLESS STEEL TONGS for turning food. Buy an extra pair for handling the coals. Once you own these, you'll never use another kind.

LONG-HANDLED PROFESSIONAL PANCAKE TURNER with 3-inch-wide, 7- to 14-inch-long blade attached to a wooden handle. You will have more control lifting food with this kind of turner than with an ordinary long-handled pancake turner.

LONG-HANDLED BASTING BRUSH with a 2- or 3-inch-wide head.

LONG-HANDLED FORK for checking the doneness of poultry and lifting the grill.

LONG-HANDLED COMBINATION WIRE BRUSH (WITH BRASS BRISTLES) AND SCRAPER for quickly cleaning burned-on bits of food from the grill rack.

PORCELAIN CLEANING BRUSH specially designed to clean, but not scratch, porcelain grids.

EXTRA-LONG OVEN MITTS.

SPRAY BOTTLE for dousing flare-ups.

SKEWERS, flat-bladed, that are either stainless steel or bamboo.

MEAT THERMOMETER.

G R I L L I N G   T I P S

To test the heat: If you can hold your hand, palm side down, about three inches above the grill for the following designated time, your grill is hot (2 seconds); medium-hot (3 seconds); medium (4 seconds); low (5 seconds).

- Remember to bring food to room temperature thirty minutes to one hour before grilling.
- Always grill first the side of the food that will be presented.
- If you are seasoning food with salt and pepper, use it just before grilling.

- Food that has been marinated, especially chicken with the skin on, is best turned often, so it can brown evenly without burning.
- Gas and electric grills don't get as hot as charcoal or wood-burning grills, so they should always be preheated at least ten to fifteen minutes before grilling to prevent food from sticking to the rack.
- Any food that has been marinated or brushed with oil can go directly on a hot grill. Otherwise, oil the grill before heating it, especially when cooking food that has been rubbed with a spice paste or is skinless, such as chicken, vegetables, and seafood.
- For safety's sake, don't grill outdoors during high winds.

GREENS BASICS

(OR SOME TIPS ON THE ICEBERG)

If you love crunch, a good first-course salad can be as plain and simple as a wedge of iceberg lettuce, decorously adorned with a few tomato slices and cloaked with Thousand Island dressing. Although, for snazzier, more eye-dazzling first courses, you can take advantage of the intriguing variety of produce—from baby lettuces to Asian greens and delicate herbs—stocked in most large supermarkets. By adding an assortment of baby vegetables, a warm or hot herb-infused grilled chicken breast, or a quickly seared fish fillet, you've made yourself an intriguing and satisfying main course. And, if you're a sandwich fancier, try filling a crusty roll or two slices of bread with your favorite salad fixings or grilled veggies.

These lovely leaves aren't limited to composed salads, or to plain steamed or boiled greens, for that matter. Iceberg or romaine leaves make dainty wrappers for low-calorie burritos or stuffed sandwiches, and quickly deep-fried baby spinach leaves, cilantro, or parsley can be transformed into the crispiest greens that are served like chips. On the trendiest menus, greens also show up as wonderful side dishes, such as warm spinach wilted with a hot bacon-balsamic vinaigrette, spicy stir-fried Italian rapini flavored with garlic, olive oil, and red pepper flakes, and grilled radicchio or endive brushed with a heady extra-virgin olive oil and served hot or at room temperature.

However they're served, healthy, flavorful greens of all kinds have found a permanent place on our plates.

HANDLING GREENS

One of the most important considerations when choosing greens is quality. Select the most beautiful and freshest-looking greens and use them as soon after purchasing (or harvesting) as possible. Handle them gently since they bruise easily.

If you're not planning to use them right away, place the greens whole and unwashed in a plastic bag with air holes or wrap in a damp towel and store them in the refrigerator. Changing the towel one or two times will keep them crisp for about a week. Herbs, which are quite perishable, should not be washed until just before use.

Gently rinse all greens under cold running water before using. Head lettuces should be cored before holding under a stream of water. The leaves of leafy greens should be separated from their core and each leaf thoroughly washed. Large leaves should be torn into bite-size pieces. Make sure you check the undersides for clinging insects or excess soil. Sandy greens, like spinach, should be submerged in a sink full of cold water, swished until clean with your hands, then rinsed and drained. Never soak greens for any length of time.

To dry, shake, blot, or pat with paper towels or use a salad spinner. (Years ago, I watched a friend who had a large family toss a bunch of greens into a clean, dry pillowcase and give them a quick spin in her washing machine. She stored the greens in the same pillowcase in her second refrigerator, where she had an empty shelf. Her system worked without damaging a leaf! I was impressed by her ingenuity and thought it was a terrific idea for preparing greens in advance for my next party.)

Wrap the washed and dried greens in paper towels to absorb any excess moisture that might accumulate, and place them in a plastic bag. Crisp in the refrigerator for an hour or two before dressing. Lettuce and other greens will keep for three to five days in the refrigerator in a plastic bag, but place them away from apples, pears, or melons. These fruits emit gases that can cause greens to turn brown.

Greens should be completely dry before being used raw in salads so that the dressing will cling to each leaf and not be diluted with excess water. Always toss greens with dressing just prior to serving or at the table.

Salad greens should not be frozen unless you're planning to use them cooked or wilted. With the exception of lettuce, all greens freeze very well. After washing, blanch them for two minutes, drain, chill in ice water for two minutes, and drain again. Pat them dry and store in Ziploc bags or airtight freezer containers. They will keep for eight to ten months. Herbs should be washed, but need not be blanched, before freezing. They will keep for six months and should be used without defrosting.

SALAD-MAKING HINTS

The younger the greens, the more tender the leaves and stalks, and the milder the flavor. All young greens are delicious tossed raw into salads or stir-fried. Baby varieties of strong-flavored greens are excellent in salads, but as the plants mature and the flavors become more intense, they're more interesting cooked your favorite way.

Most greens are interchangeable, so when creating your own mixes, balance the stronger, more pungent leaves (like turnip, arugula, and mustard greens) with those having a milder flavor (like spinach). Perk up any salad mix by adding fresh herbs.

Five ounces of raw greens will serve two to four. One large handful of greens yields about four cups, or three ounces.

SUGGESTED MIXES

ASIAN SPINACH MIX FOR RAW AND WILTED SALADS Use baby greens—cabbage, chrysanthemum, dandelion, kale, red mustard, mizuna, osaka, bok choy, peppercress, and tatsoi.

BRAISING MIX FOR WARM SALADS OR LIGHT STIR-FRY Use midsize greens—hearty and spicy baby greens like red and green chard, spinach, crimson beet tops, Savoy spinach, kale, mustard, orach, and tatsoi.

FRENCH/PROVENÇAL MIX Belgian endive, limestone lettuce, baby oak leaf, watercress, basil, chervil.

ITALIAN MIX Radicchio, arugula, romaine.

KENTER CANYON FARM'S EAST-WEST SALAD (SPICY BABY GREENS MIX) Leaf-picked tatsoi, shungiku, mizuna, purple amaranth, tiny arrow leaf spinach, purple nasturtium leaf, variegated nasturtium leaf, purple wasabe mustard, curly cress, land cress, mâche, and blond *frisée*.

MESCLUN OR FIELD MIX A mix of wild and cultivated young greens, traditional in the south of France, where it is dressed with a garlicky olive oil vinaigrette.

A good mixture has at least fifteen to eighteen kinds of greens, and never fewer than ten, including arugula and chervil and a combination of several kinds of baby greens like romaine and butter lettuce, *frisée,* lollo rossa, lollo bianco, red grenobloise, oak leaf, summer Bibb, and even edible flowers such as nasturtiums and pansies.

SOUTHERN "MESS OF GREENS" Cooked kale, turnip greens, collards, and Swiss chard, traditionally served on New Year's Day with black-eyed peas and ham for good luck. Try a raw "baby mess of greens" salad dressed with a light vinaigrette.

SPICY MIX Arugula, chervil, land and watercress, *frisée,* mâche, and radicchio.

III

VEGETABLES

SALADS

Moroccan Vegetable Salad

Crudité Grill with Pesto Mayonnaise

Chèvre and Papaya Salad on Bitter Greens

Shiitake Mushrooms on Asian Greens with Vermont Cheddar

Grilled New Potato and Asparagus Salad

Roasted Tomato Salad with Feta Cheese and Olives

Asparagus Salad with Black and White Sesame Seeds

Baby Leeks with Mint

Herbed Fusilli and Japanese Eggplant Salad

SANDWICHES

Zucchini Blossom and White Corn Quesadillas

Grilled Wild Mushrooms, Radicchio, and Sprouts Sandwich

Peppers and Eggplant Club with Fontina and Sun-Dried Tomatoes

Grilled vegetables taste delicious and are a wonderful addition to any lunch or dinner, whether they're the centerpiece of a vegetarian main course, served hot on the side, chilled in a salad tossed with a lively vinaigrette, or used at room temperature in an antipasto or a sandwich.

You can grill any of your favorite vegetables with very little advance preparation. Root vegetables, such as carrots, beets, turnips, and rutabagas, will cook quickly and more evenly if first parboiled, steamed, or briefly microwaved. Spongy vegetables, like eggplant or mushrooms—which absorb a lot of oil when sautéed—need only a light coating of oil before being quickly grilled. And greens, such as endive, fennel, and radicchio—grilled, the way they do in Italy—are transformed from everyday salad bowl vegetables into crunchy, sweet treats.

The one rule of thumb to remember is to lightly brush all vegetables with oil or bathe them in an oil-based marinade before grilling in order to keep them from drying out. From artichokes to zucchini, there isn't a vegetable that won't benefit in looks and taste from being cooked on the grill.

PRECEDING SPREAD: *Peppers and Eggplant Club with Fontina and Sun-Dried Tomatoes (page 38)*

MOROCCAN VEGETABLE SALAD

You can double the dressing and use half to marinate the vegetables before grilling if you wish. A good feta cheese or any mild goat cheese goes particularly well with this colorful salad.

DRESSING

1 cup olive oil
⅓ cup lemon juice
¼ cup chopped fresh parsley

4 garlic cloves, crushed
1 teaspoon ground cumin
   Salt and freshly ground pepper to taste

SALAD

6 red bell peppers, halved lengthwise, stems, ribs, and seeds removed
6 yellow bell peppers, halved lengthwise, stems, ribs, and seeds removed
6 green bell peppers, halved lengthwise, stems, ribs, and seeds removed
12 small Japanese eggplants, trimmed and halved lengthwise

   Olive oil
   Salt and freshly ground pepper
6 large ripe tomatoes, peeled, seeded, and diced
1 teaspoon dried red chile flakes
1 bunch cilantro, leaves only, finely chopped (about ½ cup)
   Greek or Niçoise olives for garnish

Mix together the oil, lemon juice, parsley, garlic, and cumin. Season with salt and pepper to taste. Set aside.

Grill the peppers over very hot coals for 10 to 15 minutes, or until blackened. Place in a paper or plastic bag and let steam for 10 to 15 minutes. Peel off the charred skin with your fingers or a sharp paring knife. Cut the peppers into ½-inch-wide strips. Set aside.

Rub the eggplants with olive oil and season with salt and pepper. Grill over medium-hot coals, flesh side down, for 3 to 4 minutes. Turn and grill for another 3 to 4 minutes, or until soft.

Toss the tomatoes with ½ cup of the dressing and mound them in the center of a large serving platter. Sprinkle the eggplants with the chile flakes and cilantro. Toss to mix evenly. Arrange in rows on the platter alternating with rows of the different-colored peppers. Sprinkle with the remaining dressing and garnish with the olives.

SERVES 4 TO 6

CRUDITÉ GRILL WITH PESTO MAYONNAISE

⊐ ııııⵑ

Depending on the type of grill you have, it might be easier to prevent the vegetables from falling through by cooking them on a screen or in a grill basket. We prefer to put the vegetables right on the grilling rack to achieve a restaurant-perfect look. Extra grilled vegetables will keep a day or two in the refrigerator. For a delicious impromptu sandwich, pile them high in a sliced baguette.

4   baby beets, trimmed, leaving 2 inches of greens
4   baby turnips, trimmed, leaving 2 inches of greens
2   ears of corn, husked and halved
2   yellow squash, cut into 4 wedges
2   red bell peppers, halved lengthwise, stems, ribs, and seeds removed
2   yellow bell peppers, halved lengthwise, stems, ribs, and seeds removed

2   Japanese eggplants, halved lengthwise
2   large Italian plum (Roma) tomatoes, halved lengthwise
2   green zucchini, cut into ¼-inch slices
4   scallions, both ends trimmed, leaving 3 inches of green
½   cup olive oil
    Salt and freshly ground pepper to taste
1¼ cups Pesto Mayonnaise (page 159)

Parboil the beets and turnips together for about 5 minutes in lightly salted water. Drain and refresh under cold water. Pat dry with paper toweling and cut in half.

Brush all of the vegetables with olive oil. Sprinkle with salt and pepper. Place the vegetables on a hot grill, removing them as they are done and keeping them warm. Grill as follows: corn, 15 to 20 minutes, turning once or twice; yellow squash, 10 minutes per side; peppers, skin side down, and eggplants, cut side down, about 9 minutes per side; tomatoes, beets, and turnips, cut side down, about 5 minutes per side; and zucchini and scallions, 4 to 5 minutes per side.

Arrange on a large platter and serve with Pesto Mayonnaise on the side.

SERVES 4

Crudité Grill with Pesto Mayonnaise

CHÉVRE AND PAPAYA SALAD
ON BITTER GREENS

It is very important with this recipe to use a creamy goat cheese that will slice easily rather than crumble. If you have a wire basket, the cheese can be quickly grilled on both sides on the barbecue.

SHERRY VINAIGRETTE

6 tablespoons extra-virgin olive oil
1 teaspoon kosher salt

2 tablespoons sherry wine vinegar
Freshly ground pepper

SALAD

¾ pound very cold Montrachet chèvre or other noncrumbly goat cheese
⅓ cup dry unseasoned bread crumbs
1 large or 2 small papayas, peeled, halved, and seeded
12 leaves Belgian endive

4 ounces arugula, stemmed
1 small head butter lettuce, finely shredded
2 tablespoons coarsely chopped toasted pecans

Mix the vinaigrette ingredients together in a small jar and shake well. Set aside.

Cut the chèvre into 12 slices about ½ inch thick. Sprinkle the slices with the bread crumbs, lightly pressing them into the cheese with your fingertips so that they adhere. Turn the cheese over and repeat. Chill or freeze 10 minutes.

Cut each papaya in half lengthwise into quarters. Cut each quarter lengthwise into 4 or 5 slices. Cut the slices in half crosswise. Reserve 28 of the most attractive slices. Dice the remaining papaya.

Place 4 tablespoons of the dressing in a large bowl and lightly sweep the endive through to barely coat. Save any remaining dressing. Arrange the leaves on 4 dinner plates with stems to the center. Toss the arugula, butter lettuce, and diced papaya in 2 tablespoons of the dressing. Place on top of the endive and heap into a mound. Arrange 7 papaya slices in spoke fashion around the edges of the plate.

Preheat the broiler.

Put the breaded cheese slices on a lightly oiled pan. Broil 4 to 5 inches from the heat until the crumbs are lightly browned, about 1 minute. Carefully turn each slice over with a spatula and broil an additional minute. Immediately remove from the broiler and arrange 3 slices of the cheese atop the center of each salad.

Heat the remaining dressing in a small pan over medium heat. As soon as the vinegar fumes are strong, pour over the salads. Sprinkle with the chopped pecans.

SERVES 4

SHIITAKE MUSHROOMS ON ASIAN GREENS WITH VERMONT CHEDDAR

Shiitake mushrooms have an intense, woodsy flavor and meatlike texture, and they are low in calories and high in fiber. Good-quality shiitakes will have firm, down-turned dark caps and white undersides.

6 or 8 large shiitake mushrooms, wiped clean, tough stems removed
6 tablespoons Garlic Oil, at room temperature (page **160**)
1 tablespoon balsamic vinegar
½ garlic clove, finely minced

¼ teaspoon salt
Freshly ground pepper
6 ounces mixed baby Asian greens, such as spinach, tatsoi, kale, red mustard, and mizuna
3 ounces white Vermont cheddar, cubed

Brush the mushrooms lightly with 2 tablespoons Garlic Oil. Grill over medium-high heat, rounded side down first, turning once or twice, for 5 to 10 minutes, or until just tender but not shriveled.

Meanwhile, mix the remaining oil with the vinegar, garlic, salt, and pepper.

Toss the greens and cheese with just enough dressing to coat lightly and arrange on 2 plates. Top each serving with 3 mushrooms.

SERVES 2

GRILLED NEW POTATO AND ASPARAGUS SALAD

Depending on your preference, use either Aïoli for a strong garlic flavor or the Roasted Garlic Aïoli for a mellow nutty flavor. Watch the potatoes carefully so they don't overbrown.

2 pounds new potatoes (red bliss, Yukon Gold, or purple Peruvian), scrubbed and quartered	**⅔** cup Aïoli or Roasted Garlic Aïoli (page **158**)
2 teaspoons chopped fresh garlic	**¼** cup chopped red onion
3 to 4 tablespoons olive oil	**¼** cup chopped scallions
Salt and freshly ground pepper to taste	**¼** cup chopped Marinated Sun-Dried Tomatoes (page **157**) or store-bought, packed in oil
1 pound medium-large asparagus, trimmed	**2** teaspoons chopped Italian parsley

Toss the potatoes in a large bowl with the garlic, enough oil to coat, and salt and pepper. Place on an oiled grill and cook, covered, over medium-hot heat for 10 to 15 minutes, or until the potatoes are lightly browned and tender when pierced with a fork. Turn several times with a spatula to ensure even cooking. Remove and keep warm.

Brush the asparagus with the remaining oil and season with salt and pepper. Grill, uncovered, for 5 to 7 minutes, turning frequently, until lightly browned but still crisp. When done, cut on the diagonal into 3 or 4 pieces.

Combine the remaining ingredients in a large bowl. Gently toss with the warm potatoes and the asparagus. Serve warm or at room temperature.

SERVES 4 TO 6

Grilled New Potato and Asparagus Salad

ROASTED TOMATO SALAD WITH FETA CHEESE AND OLIVES

Greek or Corsican feta cheese is slightly tangy and salty and has a creamy texture. It is traditionally made from sheep's milk that is "pickled" in brine. It's best to use a young cheese because it becomes too salty as it ages. If imported cheese is not available, use best-quality domestic feta cheese or substitute chèvre.

VINAIGRETTE

- 6 tablespoons extra-virgin olive oil
- 2 tablespoons sherry wine vinegar
- 1 teaspoon minced garlic
  Salt and freshly ground pepper

SALAD

- 4 cups (1 huge handful) arugula
- 24 Niçoise or Kalamata olives, pitted
- 2 beefsteak tomatoes, halved
  Garlic Oil (page 160)
- ¼ pound Greek or Corsican feta cheese, crumbled into large pieces
- 4 hard-cooked egg yolks, finely chopped

Mix the oil, vinegar, garlic, and salt and pepper together in a small bowl. Set aside. In a medium bowl, toss the arugula with the olives. Refrigerate if making in advance.

Brush the tomatoes with the Garlic Oil. Grill over medium heat, cut side down, for about 5 minutes. Turn and sprinkle with the feta cheese. Cover the grill and continue grilling tomatoes about 4 minutes, or just until the cheese is warmed and slightly melted. Set aside and keep warm.

Remove the arugula from the refrigerator, if chilled. Heat the vinaigrette over medium heat just until warm and toss with the greens. Arrange on 2 plates. Place the tomatoes in the center of the greens. Sprinkle with the egg yolks and serve immediately, while warm.

SERVES 2

ASPARAGUS SALAD WITH BLACK AND WHITE SESAME SEEDS

Use thin or medium-size asparagus no thicker than your little finger. If you prefer, you can omit blanching the asparagus and grill the raw spears 5 to 7 minutes over medium heat. Black sesame seeds can be purchased at Asian markets.

2 tablespoons plus 2 teaspoons sugar	1 pound asparagus
5 teaspoons rice vinegar	Peanut oil
4 teaspoons light soy sauce	2 teaspoons toasted white sesame seeds
¼ cup sesame oil	2 teaspoons black sesame seeds

Combine the sugar, vinegar, soy sauce, and sesame oil in a small bowl. Set aside.

Trim the woody ends from the asparagus. Place the spears in a large pot of boiling water and blanch for 1 minute. Drain.

Brush the asparagus with a little peanut oil. Place on an oiled grill and cook over medium heat for 4 to 5 minutes, turning to evenly mark the spears. The asparagus are done when the spears are pliable when lifted, but not mushy when pierced with a fork. Let cool and cut on the diagonal into 3 pieces.

In a large bowl, toss the asparagus with just enough dressing to coat. Chill, if desired, or serve at room temperature. Toss with the sesame seeds before serving. Any leftover dressing can be served on the side or reserved for another use.

SERVES 2 TO 4

BABY LEEKS WITH MINT

Unlike the tops of full-grown leeks, those of baby leeks are tender and delicious when cooked.

BASIL OIL VINAIGRETTE

3	tablespoons red wine vinegar	½	cup finely shredded mint leaves
2	teaspoons Dijon mustard	¼	cup diced red bell pepper
1½	teaspoons salt	¼	cup diced yellow bell pepper
¼	teaspoon freshly cracked black pepper	¼	cup Niçoise olives, pitted and chopped
9	tablespoons Basil Oil or Garlic Oil (page 160)	½	teaspoon grated lemon zest

24	baby leeks, root ends trimmed, washed		Olive oil

Whisk together the vinegar, mustard, salt, and pepper in a medium bowl. Slowly whisk in the oil until the mixture is thick. Stir in the mint, peppers, olives, and lemon zest. Set aside.

Trim off any ragged ends of the green part of the leeks. Brush the leeks with oil and grill over medium-high heat, turning to brown evenly, for 5 to 6 minutes.

Arrange the leeks on plates and drizzle with the vinaigrette. Serve warm or at room temperature.

SERVES 4

Baby Leeks with Mint

HERBED FUSILLI AND JAPANESE EGGPLANT SALAD

コ⚊⚊⚊⊏

Fresh water chestnuts, sold in the produce sections of Asian and gourmet markets, are superior to the flavorless canned ones. Place them in acidulated water when peeling to prevent discoloration.

1	pound tricolor fusilli	12	scallions, root end and ragged top trimmed
1 to 2	tablespoons safflower oil		
6	small Japanese eggplants, trimmed and halved lengthwise	¼	pound snow peas, washed and trimmed
		12	fresh water chestnuts, peeled and sliced
2 to 3	tablespoons olive oil		
1	teaspoon dried thyme	½	bunch dill (about ¼ ounce), chopped
1	large red bell pepper, split and seeded	1⅓	cups Fresh Herb and Champagne Vinaigrette (recipe follows)
			Salt and freshly ground pepper

Cook the pasta al dente according to package directions. Rinse well. Toss with safflower oil. Set aside.

Brush the eggplants with some olive oil and sprinkle with thyme. Grill, cut side down first, over medium-hot coals, 8 to 10 minutes per side. Brush the pepper with a little oil and grill about 10 minutes, turning as the skin blisters. Brush 6 scallions with oil and grill for 7 to 10 minutes, or until soft and marked.

Julienne the remaining scallions. Slice the eggplant into chunks. Scrape off any charred skin from the pepper, then cut into strips. Combine the pasta, all the vegetables except the grilled scallions, and the dill in a large bowl and toss with the vinaigrette. Adjust the seasonings. Place grilled scallions around the bowl. Serve at room temperature.

SERVES 4 TO 6

FRESH HERB AND CHAMPAGNE VINAIGRETTE

Use the lesser amount of oil if you prefer a sharper dressing.

1 shallot, peeled and quartered	Freshly ground pepper
1 garlic clove, peeled	Few drops of Tabasco sauce
1 cup loosely packed Italian parsley leaves	¾ to 1 cup peanut or light olive oil
¼ cup champagne vinegar	2 tablespoons chopped fresh chives
1½ teaspoons Dijon mustard	1 tablespoon chopped fresh basil
1 teaspoon sugar	1 tablespoon chopped fresh chervil
½ teaspoon salt	1 tablespoon chopped fresh tarragon

Securely lock the lid of a food processor bowl fitted with the metal blade. With the machine running, finely chop the shallot and garlic by dropping them through the feed tube. Add the parsley and pulse to chop. Add the vinegar, mustard, sugar, salt, pepper to taste, and Tabasco sauce. Pulse a few times to combine. With the machine running, slowly pour the oil through the feed tube, processing a couple of seconds to combine. Pour the mixture into a small bowl and stir in the remaining ingredients. Adjust seasonings to taste.

MAKES ABOUT 1⅓ TO 1½ CUPS

l l l

ZUCCHINI BLOSSOM AND
WHITE CORN QUESADILLAS

When preparing chiles, whether raw or roasted, it is wise to wear disposable rubber gloves to protect your hands. The fiery oils found in the veins and seeds of chile peppers can cause great discomfort or painful burning if you should accidentally touch your skin, mouth, or eyes.

1 large poblano or Anaheim chile pepper	**½** cup chicken stock
Corn oil	**4** large flour tortillas used for burritos
1 cup cleaned and chopped zucchini	**6** ounces Monterey Jack cheese,
blossoms	crumbled
½ cup diced zucchini	Guacamole (page 143)
½ cup fresh or frozen white corn	Pico de Gallo (page 152)

Grill the chile over very hot coals or in a flame on top of the stove until blackened, about 10 minutes. Place in a paper bag and let steam for 10 to 15 minutes. Peel off the charred skin using your fingers or a sharp paring knife. Remove the seeds and coarsely chop the chile. Set aside.

Heat 2 tablespoons oil in a large skillet over high heat. Add the blossoms, zucchini, corn, and peppers. Lower the heat to medium-high and sauté several minutes until the vegetables are soft, then add the chicken stock. Cook several minutes more over medium-high heat until all the liquid is absorbed. Let cool to warm.

To assemble the quesadilla, spread ½ cup of filling on one half side of a tortilla, keeping the filling within ¼ inch from the edge. Sprinkle with some of the cheese. Fold the other half over to close. Lightly brush the folded tortilla with a little oil. Repeat with remaining tortillas. Place quesadillas on a lightly oiled grill or grilling rack and cook, covered, over medium heat, about 45 seconds per side, just until the cheese has melted and the tortilla is lightly browned. To serve, cut each quesadilla into 4 wedges with a sharp knife or pizza cutter. Accompany with Guacamole and Pico de Gallo or your favorite spicy salsa.

SERVES 4

Grilled Wild Mushrooms, Radicchio, and Sprouts Sandwich (page 38)

GRILLED WILD MUSHROOMS, RADICCHIO, AND SPROUTS SANDWICH

⊐ I I I I ⊏

Serve this sandwich with your favorite grilled potatoes and Aïoli (page 158) on the side. Onion sprouts can usually be found in a natural foods store, but if they are not available, use your choice of sprouts.

1 pound mixed wild mushrooms (chanterelles, shiitakes, oysters, Cremini), wiped clean, tough stems removed	Salt and freshly ground pepper
	6 slices Basil Bread (page 136)
	6 large radicchio leaves
½ cup Garlic Oil (page 160) or extra-virgin olive oil	1½ to 2 cups onion sprouts

If using chanterelles and Creminis, cut them in half. Leave the shiitake and oyster mushrooms whole. Toss all the mushrooms in the oil to coat completely. Season with salt and pepper. On a well-oiled grill or grilling rack, cook the mushrooms over medium-hot coals for 3 to 9 minutes, or until soft and lightly browned, turning as necessary. Remove the mushrooms as they cook and keep warm. Brush each slice of bread on both sides with a little oil and lightly grill.

Place 2 radicchio leaves on 3 pieces of bread. Top with the mushrooms and onion sprouts. Top with the remaining bread, cut in half, and serve.

MAKES 3 SANDWICHES

PEPPERS AND EGGPLANT CLUB WITH FONTINA AND SUN-DRIED TOMATOES

⊐ I I I I ⊏

Using thin-sliced bread is a good way to reduce the size of this sandwich for those with small mouths or appetites. Black olive bread can be purchased through mail order (see Note) if it's not available at your local bakery. You may also substitute any good country loaf or sourdough that will yield oval slices. For extra zip, spread a little Black Olive Spread (page 140) over the buttered bread.

2 medium yellow bell peppers, halved
lengthwise, stems, ribs, and seeds
removed
2 medium red bell peppers, halved
lengthwise, stems, ribs, and seeds
removed
1 eggplant, cut lengthwise, about ¼ inch
thick
Olive oil
Salt and freshly ground pepper

4 oval slices black olive or sourdough
bread
Unsalted butter, at room temperature
2 oval slices pumpernickel bread
3 tablespoons Marinated Sun-Dried Tomatoes (page 157), or store-bought packed
in oil, drained and julienned
¼ pound imported fontina cheese, grated
(1 cup)
¼ cup chopped chives

Brush the peppers and eggplant with oil. Lightly season with salt and pepper. Place on a hot grill, cut side down. Once the peppers begin to cook around the edges, flatten them with the back of a spatula. Turn several times until they are lightly charred and cooked through, 10 to 15 minutes. Cook the eggplant slices about 10 minutes, turning once or twice until marked and cooked through. Remove vegetables from the grill. Peel off any blackened skin from the peppers and set aside. Remove 2 slices of eggplant for the sandwiches. Reserve the remaining slices for another use.

Place the olive or sourdough bread on the hot grill or under the broiler and lightly grill on one side. Lightly butter the ungrilled side of the olive or sourdough bread. Lightly butter both sides of the pumpernickel bread.

To assemble the sandwiches, layer 2 slices of olive or sourdough bread, buttered side up, as follows: Overlap slices of yellow bell pepper. Top with the tomatoes, eggplant, and pumpernickel bread. Overlap the red peppers on top of the pumpernickel and sprinkle equally with the cheese. Place the sandwiches under the broiler on the lowest rack and broil several minutes, until the cheese is melted and bubbly. Remove from the broiler and sprinkle with chives. Top with the remaining olive bread, buttered side down. Slice the sandwiches into thirds and serve immediately.

SERVES 2

Note: Black olive bread can be purchased from Balducci's "Shop from Home" Service, 11-02 Queens Plaza South, Long Island City, NY 11101-4908. Telephone: 800-225-3822.

POULTRY

SALADS

Goat Cheese—Stuffed Chicken Breasts with Tomato Vinaigrette

Isidoro's Calcutta Chicken

Vietnamese Chicken Salad with Two Dressings

Chicken Dijonnaise with Spinach Salad

Chinese Chicken Salad

Crunchy Duck Breast and Mango-Papaya Salad

Rosemary Chicken and Chicken Liver Brochettes on Sautéed Rapini

Grilled Quail on Baby Lettuce with Green Beans and Exotic Mushrooms

Duck Sausages on Braised Bitter Greens with Potato-Chive Cakes

SANDWICHES

Turkey Fillet Sandwich with Black Olive Spread

Irish Bacon and Turkey Burger with Roasted Garlic Aïoli

Duck Tacos

Turkey Fajitas

Turkey and Cranberry Chutney Sandwich

Chicken and Vegetable Sandwich with Cilantro Pesto

Turkey Brochettes on Grilled Chapati

Thuis chapter presents a mélange of poultry dishes inspired by cuisines from around the world. Poultry—especially chicken and turkey—is probably the most versatile of all meats because of its compatibility with an enormous variety of seasonings and flavors. When prepared on the grill, it takes on another—perhaps its best—dimension.

Most of our recipes are prepared with breast meat because it is convenient to use and can be quickly cooked. Chicken breasts are great time-savers when purchased already skinned and boned, and they are low in calories and fat. Turkey breasts are even lower in serum cholesterol and higher in protein than chicken, and are an economical choice for families who prefer only white meat.

Those preferring dark meat will love dishes like Duck Tacos and Grilled Quail on Baby Lettuce with Green Beans and Exotic Mushrooms and can substitute chicken thighs for the breast meat in Isidoro's Calcutta Chicken, Chinese Chicken Salad, and Vietnamese Chicken Salad with Two Dressings.

When cooking any bird, bring it to room temperature before grilling. The grill should always be well oiled and hot to prevent sticking. Chicken and turkey are done when the juices run clear, but game birds should be served a little pink.

PRECEDING SPREAD: *Grilled Quail on Baby Lettuce with Green Beans and Exotic Mushrooms (page 54)*

GOAT CHEESE-STUFFED CHICKEN
BREASTS WITH TOMATO VINAIGRETTE

You can stuff the chicken breasts in the morning and refrigerate them until you're ready to grill. Serve with grilled red potatoes and buttered baby carrots.

TOMATO VINAIGRETTE

2 large tomatoes, peeled, seeded, and diced	1 garlic clove, minced
6 tablespoons extra-virgin olive oil	Pinch of chopped fresh basil
2 tablespoons red wine vinegar	Pinch of chopped fresh chives
1 shallot, minced	Pinch of dried thyme
	Salt and freshly ground pepper

¼ pound fresh chèvre or goat cheese	10 basil leaves, chopped
1 tablespoon unsalted butter, softened	3 tablespoons chopped chives
¼ cup chopped and drained Marinated Sun-Dried Tomatoes (page 157)	¼ teaspoon dried thyme
¼ cup chopped Kalamata or Niçoise olives (about 18 Kalamatas or 52 Niçoise)	2 large whole chicken breasts, skin on, boned and halved
	Salt and freshly ground pepper

SALAD

⅔ cup extra-virgin olive oil	8 cups arugula and sorrel, mixed
⅓ cup red wine vinegar	1 limestone lettuce, leaves separated

Whisk together all of the vinaigrette ingredients, adjusting salt and pepper if necessary. Set aside.

In a small bowl, combine the chèvre, butter, tomatoes, olives, basil, 2 tablespoons of the chives, and the thyme. Hold each chicken breast flat on a cutting surface and cut through horizontally to make a pocket. Stuff each breast with one-quarter of the cheese mixture. Sprinkle breasts with a little salt and pepper. Grill over hot coals on a lightly oiled grill, skin side down first, about 7 minutes per side, or until the juices of the chicken run clear. Keep warm.

Combine the oil and vinegar. Season with salt and pepper. Lightly toss with the greens. Arrange the salad on 4 plates and top with the chicken. Spoon vinaigrette over the chicken and sprinkle with the remaining chopped chives.

SERVES 4

ISIDORO'S CALCUTTA CHICKEN

Isidoro Tapia, chef and kitchen manager at Gilliland's, created this version of Gerri's original dish, which has been on the menu ever since the restaurant opened in 1984. Served with rice on the side, it's wonderful for a summer buffet.

4	whole chicken breasts, skin on, boned and halved	2	onions, peeled and sliced ¼ inch thick Vegetable oil
¼	cup freshly squeezed lime juice	1	head romaine lettuce, washed and torn into large pieces
2	teaspoons turmeric		
2	teaspoons salt	2	lemons or limes, washed and cut into quarters
2	teaspoons coriander seeds		
1	teaspoon cumin seeds	2	large tomatoes, cut into quarters
2	large garlic cloves, peeled		Cilantro or mint leaves
One	1-inch piece fresh ginger, peeled		Tomato and Mint Sambal (page 149)
1	cup plain yogurt		Raita (page 139)
1	teaspoon chili powder		Summer Mango Chutney (page 156)
2	teaspoons Garam Masala (page 154)		

Wash and dry the chicken breasts. Mix the lime juice, turmeric, and salt together in a small bowl. Rub into the breasts, making sure all parts are thoroughly covered. Place the breasts in a shallow pan and marinate at room temperature for 30 minutes.

Meanwhile, place the coriander and cumin seeds in a small pan and toast over medium heat about 1 minute, or until they give off an aroma.

Place in a blender or spice grinder and add the garlic, ginger, and 2 tablespoons of the yogurt. Grind to form a smooth paste.

Pour into a bowl. Add the chili powder, Garam Masala, and remaining yogurt and mix thoroughly. Pour over the chicken, cover, and marinate at least 1 hour or overnight in the refrigerator.

Brush the onion slices on both sides with a little oil. Place the onions and chicken breasts, skin side down, on a hot, lightly oiled grill. Grill the onions, turning as necessary, 5 to 7 minutes, or until lightly browned on both sides and just tender. Remove from the grill and keep warm. Grill the breasts about 5 minutes, then rotate so the grill marks will crisscross. Grill for 2 minutes more, then turn and grill for 5 to 7 minutes.

To assemble, place torn lettuce on a large serving platter. Alternate the lemon and tomato wedges around the rim of the plate. Place the chicken breasts down the center of the plate on top of the lettuce. Garnish with grilled onions and large cilantro or mint leaves. Serve with the Tomato and Mint Sambal, Raita, and Summer Mango Chutney on the side.

SERVES 4

VIETNAMESE CHICKEN SALAD WITH TWO DRESSINGS

コ 𝐈𝐈𝐈𝐈 𝚺

The two easy dressings for this salad—a peanutty one for the noodles and a light ginger and scallion dressing for the cabbages—form a perfect marriage when combined. The salad makes an exceptional appetizer for any barbecue meal as well as an excellent main-course dish. Serve on oval dinner plates.

2 pounds Chinese egg noodles
  Peanut oil
1 cup chopped scallions, including green tops
2 tablespoons chopped fresh ginger
1 tablespoon dark sesame oil
¼ cup seasoned rice vinegar
4 large whole chicken breasts, skin on, boned and halved

1¾ cups Peanut Dressing (recipe follows)
½ large Chinese (Napa) cabbage, thinly sliced (about 8 cups)
¼ red cabbage, thinly sliced (about 4 cups)
1 large bunch cilantro, chopped
¼ cup unsalted whole roasted peanuts
  Large cilantro leaves

Cook the noodles according to package directions until soft. They should not be al dente. Drain and rinse under cold water until they are chilled. Toss with a little peanut oil to prevent sticking; set aside.

Whisk together the scallions, ginger, sesame oil, and seasoned rice vinegar in a small bowl. Set aside.

Grill the chicken over medium-hot coals on a lightly oiled grill, 6 to 7 minutes per side, or until done. Set aside to cool.

Toss the noodles with just enough Peanut Dressing to coat lightly (about ¾ cup). Combine the cabbages, chopped cilantro, and the vinegar mixture.

Arrange noodles on 8 dinner plates. Top each with ½ cup of the cabbage mixture. Remove the skin from the chicken and slice the meat diagonally into thin strips. Lay the strips across the cabbage. Sprinkle with peanuts. Place a small dollop of the remaining Peanut Dressing on each plate and garnish with large cilantro leaves.

SERVES 8

PEANUT DRESSING

½ cup seasoned rice vinegar
½ cup chunky peanut butter
2 tablespoons chopped fresh ginger
2 tablespoons dark sesame oil

2 tablespoons chopped scallion
2 tablespoons sugar
½ cup soy sauce
2 tablespoons chopped cilantro

Combine all the ingredients in a small bowl. Whisk until thick and creamy.

MAKES ABOUT 1¾ CUP

CHICKEN DIJONNAISE WITH SPINACH SALAD

⊐ııııⲥ

This classic French bistro dish is best accompanied with a crusty country loaf and a bottle of Pouilly-Fuissé or California Chardonnay. For an unusual twist, we like to make the marinade with Crema Mexicana, which is similar to crème fraîche and available in any Latin American market.

2 cups Crema Mexicana or crème fraîche
¾ cup Maille brand Dijon mustard (one 6½-
   ounce jar)
2 tablespoons Armagnac
   Salt and freshly ground pepper

2 large frying chickens (about 3 pounds
   each), skin on, washed, dried, and cut
   into eighths
   Spinach Salad (recipe follows)

In a large bowl, mix the Crema Mexicana, mustard, Armagnac, and salt and pepper to taste. Scrape into a 2-gallon Ziploc bag or a pan large enough to hold all the chicken. Add the chicken and coat well on all sides. Seal the bag or, if using a pan, cover with plastic wrap and marinate the chicken for 4 to 6 hours in the refrigerator, turning several times. Bring to room temperature before cooking.

Place the chicken, bone side down, on a lightly oiled grill and cook over medium-hot heat for 30 to 40 minutes, turning as needed, until golden brown and the juices run clear. Brush with the marinade if the chicken appears too dry while it cooks. Serve with Spinach Salad on the side.

SERVES 4

→

SPINACH SALAD

¼ pound thick-cut bacon, diced
1½ tablespoons Dijon mustard
5 tablespoons olive oil
2 tablespoons balsamic or red wine
vinegar

Salt and freshly ground pepper
2 bunches fresh spinach (about
¾ pound), trimmed, washed, and dried

Fry the bacon in a small skillet until brown and crisp. Drain on paper towels.

In a salad bowl, mix together the mustard and oil with a wooden spoon until well incorporated. Stir in the vinegar and season with salt and pepper to taste. Place the spinach on top of the dressing in the bowl.

Just before serving, quickly reheat the bacon bits in a clean, nonstick skillet, add to the salad bowl, and toss. Serve immediately with the chicken.

SERVES 4

CHINESE CHICKEN SALAD

This is an easy salad to put together. It can be toted to a picnic or potluck and assembled at the last minute. The dressing and the mai fun noodles (available in most Asian groceries and supermarkets) can be prepared up to a week in advance. Some supermarkets sell the noodles already prepared. The dressing should be refrigerated, but the noodles will keep at room temperature stored in an airtight plastic bag.

3 cups peanut oil
2 ounces mai fun noodles (Chinese rice vermicelli)
4 large whole chicken breasts, skinned and boned
1 head iceberg or romaine lettuce, cored and shredded
1 cup bean sprouts, sprout ends removed
6 scallions, with green tops, chopped

1 carrot, scraped and julienned
½ red bell pepper, stemmed, seeded, and julienned
½ yellow bell pepper, stemmed, seeded, and julienned
½ cup shredded red cabbage
¼ cup toasted slivered almonds or pine nuts
⅔ cup Sesame Plum Dressing (recipe follows)

Heat the oil to very hot (about 350°F. to 375°F.) in a wok. Deep-fry the noodles in small batches until they puff, 1 to 2 seconds. Drain on paper towels. Set aside.

Rub the chicken breasts with a little oil and grill over medium-high heat on a lightly oiled grill, about 6 minutes per side. Let cool slightly, then slice into shreds.

In a large salad bowl, toss together the lettuce, bean sprouts, scallions, carrot, peppers, cabbage, almonds, and ⅓ cup of the dressing. Add the noodles and enough remaining dressing to moisten, then toss lightly and arrange on 4 dinner plates. Top with the sliced chicken and serve immediately.

SERVES 4

SESAME PLUM DRESSING

This dressing can be easily doubled and made in advance.

2 tablespoons plum sauce	1 tablespoon sake
2 tablespoons Hoisin sauce	1 tablespoon seasoned rice vinegar
2 tablespoons sugar	1 teaspoon dry mustard
½ tablespoon dark sesame oil	1 teaspoon hot chili oil (optional)

Whisk all the ingredients together in a small bowl. Refrigerate until ready to use.

MAKES ⅔ CUP

III

CRUNCHY DUCK BREAST AND
MANGO-PAPAYA SALAD

⊐ ⅢⅢ ⊏

Fried wontons add crunch and extra volume to this huge main-course salad. They can be made in advance and stored overnight in a plastic bag.

HERB RUB

¾ teaspoon kosher salt

1 shallot, minced

1 teaspoon chopped Italian parsley

¼ teaspoon crushed bay leaf

Pinch of dried thyme

½ tablespoon freshly ground pepper

1 garlic clove, minced

4 (5-ounce) duck breasts, boned, skin on

SALAD

4 cups peanut oil

15 wonton wrappers, each cut into six ½-inch strips

½ pound small snow peas, stems and strings removed

12 ounces mixed baby greens

1 red pepper, stemmed, peeled, seeded, and julienned

1 yellow pepper, stemmed, peeled, seeded, and julienned

¾ cup toasted slivered almonds

¾ cup Sweet Ginger and Garlic Dressing (recipe follows)

2 large mangoes, peeled and sliced

1 large ripe papaya, peeled and thinly sliced

Mix the herb-rub ingredients together thoroughly and rub over the duck breasts. Place the breasts in a plastic bag and refrigerate overnight.

To make the salad, heat the oil to very hot (350° F. to 375° F.) in a wok. Fry the wonton strips in small batches until golden brown, 1 minute or less. Drain on paper towels. Set aside.

Blanch the snow peas in boiling water to cover just until bright green, about 10 seconds. Drain immediately and plunge peas into a bowl of ice water to refresh. Drain, pat dry, and refrigerate in an airtight bag if not being used immediately.

Bring breasts to room temperature. Grill, skin side down, over very hot coals, turning once, on a lightly oiled grill, 7 to 8 minutes for medium rare. Remove from the grill and allow to cool slightly.

Meanwhile, place the snow peas, greens, peppers, and almonds in a large salad bowl. Toss well with half the dressing. Taste and add more dressing if needed. Gently toss in the wontons, being careful not to crush them.

Remove the skin from the duck breasts and slice the meat in long, thin slices across the grain. Arrange the salad on 4 plates and fan the breasts out on top of the salad. Garnish with mango and papaya slices.

SERVES 4

SWEET GINGER AND GARLIC DRESSING

¼ cup seasoned rice vinegar
2 tablespoons soy sauce
2 tablespoons dark sesame oil
2 tablespoons Hoisin sauce
3 tablespoons sugar

1 teaspoon dry mustard
1 teaspoon chili sauce
2 tablespoons minced fresh ginger
3 garlic cloves, minced

Whisk all the ingredients together in a small bowl. Refrigerate until ready to use.

MAKES ABOUT ¾ CUP

▮▮▮

ROSEMARY CHICKEN AND CHICKEN LIVER BROCHETTES ON SAUTÉED RAPINI

Rapini, also known as rape and broccoli rabe, is a sharply flavored, bitter green (canola oil is made from the seeds) popular in Italian cooking. This dish is equally good made with turkey breast fillets or medallions, grilled pork tenderloin, or any style of Italian sausage in place of chicken breasts.

8 to 12	large rosemary branches	1	pound chicken livers, halved, membranes removed
	Juice of 2 large lemons		
7	tablespoons virgin or extra-virgin olive oil	6	ounces thinly sliced pancetta, prosciutto, or bacon
2	teaspoons finely chopped fresh rosemary	4	whole chicken breasts, skinned, boned, and cut into 2-inch pieces
2	teaspoons finely chopped garlic	2	pounds rapini, large stems trimmed
¼	teaspoon salt	4	garlic cloves, halved
¼	teaspoon freshly ground pepper	2	tablespoons pine nuts
		¼	teaspoon crushed red pepper flakes

To make skewers, closely trim the leaves of the rosemary branches to about ¼ inch. Leave about 2 inches at the uncut end of the branches untrimmed. Soak the skewers in a pan of water large enough to accommodate the branches for about 20 minutes before using.

In a small bowl, combine the lemon juice, 4 tablespoons of the oil, fresh rosemary, chopped garlic, salt, and pepper. Set aside.

Wrap the chicken livers completely in the pancetta. Alternately thread the livers and chicken pieces onto the rosemary skewers. Brush with half the marinade or pour half the marinade into a long dish and marinate the brochettes at room temperature for ½ hour before grilling. Place on a lightly oiled grill and cook, covered, over hot or medium-hot coals for 10 to 12 minutes, or, uncovered, about 15 minutes, turning and basting frequently with the remaining marinade until the livers are evenly browned, firm, and slightly pink inside when cut and until the chicken is no longer pink inside. Remove from the grill and keep warm.

Meanwhile, wash the rapini, but do not dry it completely. Cut into 1-inch pieces. Heat the remaining oil in a large skillet over medium heat. Add the garlic cloves and sauté for 1 minute, then add the rapini, pine nuts, and pepper flakes. (This might have to be done in 2 batches.) Cook for 3 to 4 minutes, or until the rapini is tender and wilted, stirring frequently. Season with salt and pepper.

Divide the rapini among 4 plates. Arrange 2 or 3 skewers on top and serve immediately.

SERVES 4

Rosemary Chicken and Chicken Liver Brochettes on Sautéed Rapini

GRILLED QUAIL ON BABY LETTUCE WITH GREEN BEANS AND EXOTIC MUSHROOMS

⊐ㅣㅣㅣ⊏

If you can find the slim French green beans (haricots verts), baby green beans, or even Chinese long beans, use them instead of regular green beans for a more elegant-looking dish.

DRESSING

¾ cup olive oil

⅓ cup balsamic vinegar

1 shallot, minced

Salt and freshly ground pepper

SALAD

½ pound green beans, ends trimmed

4 quail, cleaned and breastbone removed

6 tablespoons olive oil

Salt and freshly ground pepper

1 tablespoon unsalted butter

¾ pound mixed large exotic mushrooms, wiped clean and tough stems removed

12 ounces baby lettuces

½ cup toasted pecans

Whisk together the dressing ingredients in a small bowl. Set aside.

Bring a large pot of slightly salted water to a boil. Add the beans, bring the water back to a boil, and cook beans for 3 to 4 minutes, or until bright green. Do not overcook. Drain immediately and plunge beans into a bowl of ice water to refresh. Drain, pat dry, and set aside.

Rub each quail with 1 tablespoon olive oil. Sprinkle with salt and pepper to taste. Grill over very hot coals on a lightly oiled grill, turning occasionally, until the skin is golden brown and the breast meat is barely pink, 8 to 10 minutes. Set aside, covered, to keep warm.

Heat the butter and remaining olive oil in a skillet. Sauté the mushrooms until soft, then add 1 tablespoon dressing and quickly warm.

Toss the lettuces with just enough dressing to lightly coat the leaves. Toss in most of the beans, reserving 4 little bundles for garnish. Sprinkle in the mushrooms, working quickly so the greens don't wilt.

Arrange the greens on 4 plates. Place a quail, breast side up, in the center. Place a bundle of beans at the base of each plate. Sprinkle with toasted pecans.

SERVES 4

DUCK SAUSAGES ON BRAISED BITTER GREENS WITH POTATO-CHIVE CAKES

⊐Ⅰ Ⅰ Ⅰ ⊏

Duck sausage is available at gourmet markets or through mail-order sausage companies (see Note). The accompanying Potato-Chive Cakes can be made ahead and kept warm in the oven.

DRESSING

4 tablespoons extra-virgin olive oil

1 tablespoon balsamic vinegar

½ shallot, minced

Salt and freshly ground pepper

SALAD

4 duck sausages (about 1 pound)

3½ tablespoons olive oil

1 tablespoon chopped garlic

1½ pounds mixed bitter greens (such as red and green chard leaves, spinach, chicory, crimson beet tops, and other hearty greens)

1 teaspoon balsamic vinegar

½ teaspoon salt

Freshly ground pepper

¼ cup toasted walnut or pecan halves

Potato-Chive Cakes (page 140)

Whisk together the dressing ingredients in a small bowl until well combined. Set aside.

Grill the sausages over medium-hot coals on a lightly oiled grill for 12 to 15 minutes, turning frequently to ensure even browning. Remove from the grill and keep warm.

Heat the olive oil and garlic in a large (12-inch) skillet or wok. Place all the greens in the hot pan and quickly sauté over high heat for 2 or 3 minutes. Don't worry about them overflowing. The greens will shrink very fast as they cook.

Off the heat, sprinkle the greens with the balsamic vinegar, 3 tablespoons of the dressing, and salt and pepper to taste. Quickly stir over high heat just until the greens absorb the dressing.

Arrange the greens in the center of individual dinner plates. Sprinkle with the walnuts. Slice the sausages on an angle into ½-inch pieces and arrange down the center of the greens. Serve with Potato-Chive Cakes.

SERVES 4   →

Note: Duck sausages can be mail-ordered from Aidel's Sausage Company, 1575 Minnesota Street, San Francisco, CA 94107. Telephone: 415-285-6660.

Variation

For a sandwich, stuff the greens and sausage slices into warmed pita bread or a slightly hollowed-out Italian roll.

TURKEY FILLET SANDWICH WITH BLACK OLIVE SPREAD

Turkey fillet is the tenderloin of the turkey breast. Since this lean cut grills quickly, watch carefully so that it doesn't overcook and become too dry. According to the National Turkey Federation, you can cut the cooking time in half by butterflying the tenderloins.

1½ pounds turkey fillets (3 or 4 fillets) Olive oil Salt and freshly ground pepper	4 small Italian plum (Roma) tomatoes, sliced
8 slices herb or crusty country bread	6 tablespoons Black Olive Spread (page 140)
¼ cup Mayonnaise (page 159)	Chopped chives
16 large basil leaves, thinly shredded	Rosemary branches
16 large arugula leaves, thinly shredded	Orange sections

Rub the turkey fillets with a little olive oil. Sprinkle with salt and pepper to taste. Grill on a lightly oiled grill over medium-high heat for 10 to 15 minutes, turning once or twice to evenly mark the meat. Remove from the grill and let stand 5 minutes.

Spread 4 slices of bread with Mayonnaise. Arrange the basil and arugula on top, then add the tomato slices. Spread the remaining bread with the Black Olive Spread. Slice the turkey fillets on the diagonal. Place on the bread with Black Olive Spread and sprinkle with chives. Serve open-faced or closed. Garnish the plate with rosemary branches and orange sections.

SERVES 4

IRISH BACON AND TURKEY BURGER
WITH ROASTED GARLIC AÏOLI

Irish bacon is cut much thicker than ordinary American bacon, but is less salty and has fewer calories. It is available at specialty food stores.

1½ pounds ground turkey (or chicken, if you wish)	Olive oil
2 tablespoons chopped parsley	4 burger buns, or sourdough, kaiser, or onion rolls
¼ teaspoon ground white pepper	Roasted Garlic Aïoli (page 158)
8 slices Irish bacon	

SUGGESTED ACCOMPANIMENTS

Mixed field greens	Agustine's Tomatillo Salsa Cruda (page 151)
Watercress	Apple-Tomatillo Salsa (page 147)
Tomatoes	Sweet Potato Chips or French-Fried Sweet
Roasted red peppers	Potatoes (page 142)

Mix the turkey with the parsley and pepper. Gently form into 4 large patties, being careful not to pack them too tightly.

Lightly pound the bacon between 2 pieces of plastic wrap to flatten. Wrap 2 pieces of bacon around each burger, securing with toothpicks if necessary. Cook the burgers on a lightly oiled grill rack over medium-hot coals for 6 to 10 minutes per side, or until the meat is not pink in the center, the juices run clear, and the internal temperature reaches 165° F. on a meat thermometer.

Split the rolls and spread each side with a little Roasted Garlic Aïoli before inserting the burger. Serve with your favorite accompaniments.

SERVES 4

Variation: Seafood Burgers

Replace the turkey with coarsely chopped or ground raw tuna or salmon. Replace the parsley with a combination of chopped scallions and chives and proceed with the above recipe. Cook on an oiled grill over medium-hot coals 4 to 6 minutes per side for medium rare, or until the desired doneness.

DUCK TACOS

Duck transforms an ordinary taco into an offbeat yet elegant main course. For a large party, make a mixed grill of chicken, turkey, and duck breasts. If you don't wish to render the duck fat yourself, goose or chicken fat can be purchased at European delis and meat markets, or through mail order (see Note). The small amount of duck fat used to refry the beans vastly improves their flavor. Any unused duck or goose fat will last indefinitely stored in a well-sealed container in the refrigerator.

1½ cups dried black beans or 2 (16-ounce) cans black beans	1 bunch cilantro, leaves only, coarsely chopped
2 tablespoons duck, goose, or chicken fat	2 large tomatoes, cored and diced
2 tablespoons olive oil	1 sweet white or red onion, sliced into rings
¼ medium onion, finely chopped (about ¼ cup)	1 cup Guacamole (page 143)
4 duck breasts, skin on	1 cup Agustine's Tomatillo Salsa Cruda (page 151)
Salt and freshly ground pepper	1 cup Pico de Gallo (page 152)
8 to 12 small soft corn tortillas	

If using dried black beans, cook according to package directions, just until soft but not mushy. Drain well, reserving about ¼ cup liquid. If using canned black beans, drain and rinse under cold water, reserving about ¼ cup liquid.

Heat the duck fat and oil in a large nonstick skillet. Sauté the chopped onions until soft and translucent. Add 1 cup of beans and the reserved liquid. Over high heat, mash the beans lightly as you fry. Continue adding the remaining beans, mashing until the beans begin to dry and pull away from the sides of the pan. Keep warm until ready to assemble the tacos.

Sprinkle the breasts with salt and pepper to taste. Grill, skin side down, on a lightly oiled grill over medium-hot coals until rare, 6 to 7 minutes per side. Remove from the grill and let rest a few minutes. Remove the skin and slice the meat into ¼-inch pieces.

Meanwhile, wrap the tortillas in foil and place on the hot grill to warm. They heat faster in a covered grill.

Place the sliced duck breast in the center of a large serving platter. Surround it with little piles of cilantro, tomatoes, sliced onions, Guacamole, and the refried beans. Serve with warmed tortillas and Agustine's Tomatillo Salsa Cruda and Pico de Gallo on the side.

SERVES 4

Note: Domestic duck and French goose fat can be ordered from Van Rex Gourmet Foods, Inc., 5850 Washington Blvd., Culver City, CA 90232. Telephone: 213-965-1320.

Variation: Yellowtail Tacos

Replace the duck with 1 to 1½ pounds yellowtail or any meaty fish. Grill the fish on a lightly oiled grill over high heat, 6 to 10 minutes depending on thickness, or until medium rare. Slice into bite-size pieces.

▎▎▎

FOLLOWING SPREAD: *Duck Tacos (opposite), Turkey Fajitas (page 62), Agustine's Tomatillo Salsa Cruda (page 151), and Pico de Gallo (page 152)*

TURKEY FAJITAS

Fajitas (pronounced fa-HEE-tuhs) are real cowboy food that originally were made with skirt steaks. Here, we use turkey breast tenderloins for a lighter meal.

MARINADE

1½ cups grapefruit juice	5 garlic cloves, finely minced
½ cup lime juice	1 teaspoon ground cumin
⅓ cup gold tequila	½ teaspoon chili powder
¼ cup safflower or other oil	¼ teaspoon freshly ground pepper

FAJITAS

3 pounds turkey breast tenderloins, butterflied, or boneless chicken breasts	2 yellow bell peppers, stems, ribs, and seeds removed, sliced
1 large white onion, cut into ½-inch-thick slices	2 red bell peppers, stems, ribs, and seeds removed, sliced
1 large yellow onion, cut into ½-inch-thick slices	20 scallions, root end trimmed and green tops left on
	30 medium flour tortillas

4 cups Guacamole (page 143)	2 cups sour cream
4 cups Pico de Gallo (page 152)	Chopped cilantro

In a large plastic bag, thoroughly combine the grapefruit and lime juices, tequila, oil, garlic, cumin, chili powder, and pepper. Add the turkey and onions, seal the bag, and marinate in the refrigerator for 3 to 4 hours, turning several times.

Bring the turkey to room temperature. Before cooking, remove the onions from the marinade. Brush the peppers and scallions with a little oil. Place the vegetables in a grill basket or on an oiled grill. Cook over hot coals or a combination of mesquite wood and coals for 3 to 10 minutes, turning several times, until soft. Move the vegetables to the side of the grill as they cook or remove and keep warm. Place the turkey in the center of a lightly oiled grill. Grill for 5 to 6 minutes per side (3 to 5 minutes per side for chicken), until the meat is no longer pink in the center. Wrap the tortillas in foil and warm over the grill while the turkey and vegetables cook.

Remove the turkey to a cutting board and cut the tenderloins against the grain into bite-size strips. Toss with the peppers and onions. For a buffet, serve on a large heated platter topped with the scallions, accompany with tortillas,

Guacamole, Pico de Gallo, sour cream, and cilantro, and allow guests to assemble ingredients. To serve individually, place a small amount of fajitas down the center of a tortilla, add a dollop of each condiment, and roll up. Garnish with scallions.

SERVES 8 TO 10

Variation: Beef Fajitas

Replace the turkey with 3 pounds skirt steaks cut into 6- or 8-inch steaks. Marinate for 24 hours, covered, in the refrigerator. Grill the meat for 3 to 5 minutes per side, depending on the thickness, for rare to medium rare. Let the meat stand for 5 minutes, then cut across the grain into thin slices before serving.

TURKEY AND CRANBERRY CHUTNEY SANDWICH

For this recipe, you can use either turkey cutlets or steaks, which are cut from the whole breast. The cutlets are about ¼ inch thick, the steaks about ¾ inch thick. Both are very lean and cook fast.

4 large turkey cutlets or turkey steaks	¼ cup Mayonnaise (page 159)
Vegetable oil	4 ruffled lettuce leaves
Salt and freshly ground pepper	1 cup onion or alfalfa sprouts
½ cup Cranberry Chutney (page 150)	4 tomato slices
4 onion or kaiser rolls, sliced in half	

Rub the turkey cutlets or steaks with a little oil. Sprinkle with salt and pepper. Grill the cutlets no more than 2 minutes per side, steaks for 7 to 8 minutes per side, or until the meat is no longer pink in the center, on a lightly oiled grill. Spread about 2 tablespoons Cranberry Chutney on the top half of each roll. Spread a little Mayonnaise on the bottom half and top with lettuce leaves, sprouts, tomatoes, and turkey. Close, slice in half, and serve.

SERVES 4

CHICKEN AND VEGETABLE SANDWICH WITH CILANTRO PESTO

ᴐ ၊၊၊ ᴄ

Present this sandwich for a delightful lunch or brunch entrée. The cilantro pesto adds a taste of the Southwest, but if you prefer, use basil pesto (page 161) for a Mediterranean touch. This sandwich also looks pretty if the grilled chicken breast is sliced and fanned across the bread.

1 medium eggplant, cut lengthwise ¼ inch thick	4 slices country or sourdough bread
2 slices red onion, ¼ inch thick	2 to 3 tablespoons cilantro pesto (page 161)
Olive oil	4 leaves red or butter lettuce
1 large whole chicken breast, skin on, boned and halved	6 slices tomato (1 whole)
Salt and freshly ground pepper	½ avocado, thinly sliced
	Cilantro leaves
	Yellow pearl or cherry tomatoes

Brush the eggplant and onion with olive oil. Season the vegetables and chicken with salt and pepper. Over medium-hot coals, grill the onion for 10 to 15 minutes and the eggplant for 6 to 8 minutes, or until soft. Choose 2 large slices of eggplant, reserving the rest for another use. Grill the chicken, skin side down first, on a lightly oiled grill for 6 to 7 minutes per side, until brown and the juices run clear. When done, remove the skin from the chicken.

Meanwhile, rub one side of each slice of bread with a little olive oil. Lightly grill the bread, oiled side down, then remove from the grill and spread a thin layer of pesto on the ungrilled side.

Layer 2 slices of bread with the lettuce, tomato slices, onion slices, eggplant, and chicken. Fan avocado slices over the other slice of bread. Garnish with cilantro leaves and tomatoes. Serve with a green salad or french fries.

SERVES 2

Chicken and Vegetable Sandwich with Cilantro Pesto

TURKEY BROCHETTES ON GRILLED CHAPATI

The flavors of Indian and Thai cuisine are merged in our accompaniments for the brochettes: a spicy Thai-influenced peanut sauce, Indian chapati flatbread, and Chunky Eggplant Salad. If you prefer, you can replace the chapati with an aromatic Basmati rice pilaf.

LIME-COCONUT MARINADE

½ cup canned coconut milk

¼ cup peanut oil

¼ cup chopped cilantro leaves

¼ cup fresh lime juice

4 garlic cloves, minced

1 teaspoon minced fresh ginger

1 jalapeño chile, seeded and chopped

2 tablespoons sugar

2 teaspoons Garam Masala (page 154)

2 teaspoons ground cumin

2 teaspoons ground coriander

2 teaspoons salt

1 teaspoon turmeric

BROCHETTES

1 boneless turkey breast (about 4 pounds), cut into 1-inch pieces

2 large onions, cut into 1-inch wedges

16 Chapati, store-bought or homemade (page 137)

Chunky Eggplant Salad (page 138)

2 cups Spicy Garlic and Ginger Peanut Sauce (recipe follows)

Cilantro leaves

Combine all the ingredients for the marinade in a large bowl. Pour into a Ziploc bag and add the turkey. Seal and gently rotate to coat. Marinate for 3 hours in the refrigerator, turning occasionally to distribute the marinade.

Have 16 stainless steel or bamboo skewers ready. If using bamboo skewers, remember to soak them in water for 15 to 20 minutes before threading. Alternately thread the turkey and onion pieces about ½ inch apart on the skewers. Place on a lightly oiled grill and cook over medium-high heat for 12 to 15 minutes, or until the turkey is cooked through, brushing with the marinade and turning to grill evenly. Remove to a platter and keep warm.

Grill the chapati for 2 minutes on each side. Serve the skewers on the chapati, accompanied with little bowls of Chunky Eggplant Salad and Spicy Garlic and Ginger Peanut Sauce on the side. Garnish with cilantro leaves.

SERVES 8

SPICY GARLIC AND GINGER PEANUT SAUCE

2	tablespoons peanut oil	**½**	cup coconut milk
1	cup chopped onion	**⅓**	cup *nam pla* (Thai fish sauce)
¼	cup minced garlic	**3**	tablespoons fresh lime juice
¼	cup minced fresh ginger	**6**	tablespoons sugar
½	tablespoon dried red chile flakes	**1**	cup smooth peanut butter
1	teaspoon ground cumin	**¼**	cup chopped cilantro leaves

Heat the oil in a medium frying pan over medium heat. Sauté the onion, garlic, ginger, chile flakes, and cumin until lightly browned, 6 to 8 minutes.

In a small bowl, combine the coconut milk, *nam pla,* lime juice, and sugar, stirring well. Stir in the peanut butter and add to the mixture in the pan. Cook over medium-low heat, about 5 minutes, constantly stirring to prevent the sauce from sticking. (If the sauce cooks up too thick, it can be lightly thinned with a little water or chicken stock.)

Remove from heat and let cool. Stir in the chopped cilantro. Serve warm or at room temperature. This sauce is also good with grilled chicken.

MAKES ABOUT 2 CUPS

▌▐▌

M E A T

S A L A D S

New York Strip Steak with Mushroom and Watercress Salad

Skirt Steaks with Avocado-Stuffed Chiles

Filet Mignon Caesar Salad

Marinated Beef Fillets with Chile-Lime Dressing

Thai Lamb Salad

Papas Misto with Red Leaf Lettuce and Cilantro Salad

Lavender Lamb with Warm Mushroom Salad

Lamb and Vegetable Kabobs with Grilled Red Pepper Sauce and Fennel Salad

Lemon Lamb Kabobs with Tabbouleh

Pork Loin with Celery Root, Corn, and Shiitake Salad

Chinese Orange Carnitas

Barbecued Pork Tenderloin Salad

S A N D W I C H E S

Gorgonzola Cheeseburger on Garlic-Rosemary Focaccia

Teriyaki Rib Eye Steak Dip

Carne Asada Torta

Sausage and Polenta Sandwich with Dried and Fresh Tomato-Herb Relish

Balsamic-Rosemary Lamb Sandwich with Red Onion Confit

Tenderloin of Beef and Hummus Sandwich

Т he seductive aroma of meat cooking on the grill promises a gustatory experience that is fulfilled at the first succulent bite. Flavored by the smoke of the coals and perhaps a spicy marinade or some aromatic herbs, meats such as beef, lamb, and pork have a natural affinity for the grill.

We've included a variety of marinades and sauces for the many lean cuts of meat used in this chapter. These marinades prevent the meat from drying out while cooking. And since most of them contain some kind of acid flavoring, such as citrus juices, vinegar, or wine, they also tenderize. Always marinate in a nonreactive pan, such as glass, stainless steel, or ceramic; bring meat to room temperature before cooking; and remember to pat the meat dry on paper towels before placing it on the oiled grill.

Use tongs instead of a fork when turning meat to avoid the loss of natural juices. When cooking burgers, use a spatula to turn and, please, never flatten them by pressing the back of the spatula into the burger.

PRECEDING SPREAD: *New York Strip Steak with Mushroom and Watercress Salad (opposite)*

NEW YORK STRIP STEAK WITH MUSHROOM AND WATERCRESS SALAD

These steaks are for those with hefty appetites, but two conservative eaters can share one. Slice the cheese while cold, then let it warm to room temperature. A huge baked potato is the perfect companion for this very American meal.

HONEY-MUSTARD VINAIGRETTE

2 tablespoons sherry wine vinegar
2 tablespoons grainy mustard
1 teaspoon Dijon mustard

1 tablespoon honey
1 cup peanut oil
   Salt and freshly ground pepper

SALAD

6 cups watercress, lightly packed
2 cups bean sprouts, trimmed
16 large white mushrooms, sliced
8 cherry tomatoes, halved

4 (10-ounce) New York strip steaks, about
      1½ inches thick
¼ pound Stilton cheese, sliced

To make the vinaigrette, whisk together the vinegar, mustards, and honey in a small bowl. Slowly whisk in the oil. Season with salt and pepper to taste. Set aside.

Toss together the watercress, bean sprouts, mushrooms, and tomatoes and refrigerate until ready to use.

Brush both sides of the meat with a little of the vinaigrette. Sprinkle with salt and pepper and cook on an open grill over medium-hot coals, 5 to 6 minutes per side for medium rare. Just before done, place a slice of cheese on top of the meat, cover the grill, and melt the cheese, about 1 minute. Remove the steaks to plates.

Toss the salad with just enough vinaigrette to coat lightly. Serve on separate salad plates with the steak and baked potatoes.

SERVES 4

SKIRT STEAKS WITH AVOCADO-STUFFED CHILES

⊐ ｜｜｜⊏

Queso fresco is a fresh white cheese similar to pot cheese and is available at Latin American markets or specialty cheese shops.

2½ pounds skirt steaks or flank steak, trimmed
6 Chiles in Orange Escabèche (page 153)
6 small avocados, preferably Haas
Juice of 1 lime
⅓ cup chopped cilantro leaves

Salt
1 medium head butterhead or limestone lettuce, washed and dried
¼ pound crumbled queso fresco
Grilled Onion and Garlic Relish (page 150)
Cilantro leaves

Place the meat in a shallow, nonreactive pan.

Remove the chiles from the marinade and set aside. Pour the marinade through a strainer over the meat, reserving the onions and garlic for another use. Marinate the meat for 45 minutes at room temperature.

Pit and peel the avocados. In a medium bowl, mash the avocados and the lime juice with a fork just until chunky. Stir in the cilantro and season with salt to taste.

Carefully stuff each chile with the avocado. (If any of the chiles split while stuffing, just roll up and serve seam side down.) Pinch the ends of the chiles closed so the avocado mixture doesn't discolor. Arrange a few lettuce leaves on 6 plates and top with a stuffed chile and a little cheese. Set aside.

Remove the steak from the marinade and grill over medium-hot coals for 3 to 5 minutes per side, depending on thickness, for medium rare. Remove to a cutting board and let rest a few minutes. Slice the meat about ¼ inch thick on an angle across the grain and place the slices next to the chiles. Top meat with the Grilled Onion and Garlic Relish. Garnish with cilantro leaves. Serve immediately.

SERVES 6

Skirt Steaks with Avocado-Stuffed Chiles

FILET MIGNON CAESAR SALAD

Italian chef Caesar Cardini would probably be amazed by the countless variations of his famed salad since its creation in the early 1920s.

1 medium head chilled romaine lettuce, washed and dried

1 large head chilled radicchio, washed and dried

DRESSING

1 teaspoon salt
1 garlic clove, peeled and crushed
1 teaspoon anchovy paste
1 tablespoon fresh lemon juice
½ teaspoon dry mustard
6 drops Tabasco sauce

4 (6-ounce) fillets of beef, about 2 inches thick
Salt and freshly ground pepper

1 large egg, boiled for 1 minute
3 tablespoons olive oil
2 tablespoons freshly grated Parmesan cheese
1 cup croutons

Tear the romaine and radicchio into bite-size pieces. Chill until ready to serve.

Bring the steaks to room temperature and season with salt and pepper. Grill over hot coals 6 to 8 minutes per side for rare. Let the meat rest while preparing the salad.

Sprinkle about ½ teaspoon salt in the bottom of a wooden salad bowl. Rub the bowl with the crushed garlic. Add the anchovy paste, lemon juice, mustard, remaining salt, and Tabasco sauce and whisk together. Separate the egg, reserving the white for another use if you wish. Whisk in the egg yolk, then slowly pour in the olive oil, whisking to combine well.

Add the greens, cheese, and croutons and toss. Arrange on 4 dinner plates. Slice the fillets about ¼ inch thick on an angle, and place on top of the salad. Serve immediately.

SERVES 4

MARINATED BEEF FILLETS WITH CHILE-LIME DRESSING

⊐ ╻╻╻ ⊏

The marinade for this recipe works well with any meat or poultry. Tiny black chia seeds are sold in packets at health food stores and Latin American markets. If you can't find them, omit them from the recipe.

MARINADE

½	cup plum sauce	1	tablespoon minced fresh ginger
¼	cup plum wine	2	teaspoons minced garlic
1½	tablespoons soy sauce	1	tablespoon rice vinegar
½	cup loosely packed cilantro leaves	½	tablespoon honey
2	scallions, ends trimmed, chopped	1	jalapeño chile, seeds removed, minced

4	(6-ounce) filets mignons, about 1½ inches thick	¾	cup Chile-Lime Dressing (recipe follows)
12	ounces mixed baby greens		Chia seeds

Mix all the marinade ingredients in a medium bowl. Place the beef in a Ziploc bag or nonreactive shallow pan and pour the marinade over the beef, turning to coat well. Marinate at least 1 hour but no longer than 6 hours, at room temperature.

Grill over medium-hot coals, 5 to 6 minutes per side, for medium rare.

To serve, toss the greens with just enough dressing to coat the leaves (about 2 tablespoons). Arrange on 4 dinner plates. Slice the beef on an angle into ¼-inch-thick slices and overlap them down the center of the greens. Sprinkle with a few chia seeds. Serve the remaining dressing on the side.

SERVES 4 →

CHILE-LIME DRESSING

Chinese-style chili-garlic paste is available at Asian markets and in the Asian food sections of large supermarkets.

2 tablespoons seasoned rice vinegar
2 tablespoons freshly squeezed lime juice
1 tablespoon chia seeds
¼ cup warm water
¼ cup honey

1 tablespoon Chinese-style chili-garlic paste
½ tablespoon chopped cilantro
1 small jalapeño chile, seeded and minced
1 small shallot, minced
1 large garlic clove, minced

Mix all the ingredients together in a small glass bowl. Cover and refrigerate for about 1 hour.

MAKES ABOUT ¾ CUP

THAI LAMB SALAD

⊐ııııⅭ

This makes a delicious light entrée for lunch or dinner, or it can be served as part of a buffet.

2 (6-ounce) lamb fillets
4 small garlic cloves, minced
¼ cup olive oil
  Salt and freshly ground pepper
1 red bell pepper, stem, ribs, and seeds removed, quartered
1 yellow bell pepper, stem, ribs, and seeds removed, quartered

1 large zucchini, cut into 12 (¼-inch-thick) slices
½ pound baby greens
½ cup peeled, seeded, and diced tomato
¼ cup chopped scallions
2 spears Belgian endive, coarsely chopped
  Thai Lime-Mint Dressing (recipe follows)
1 Anaheim chile, roasted, peeled, seeded, and julienned

Using a small, sharp knife, remove the thin membrane on one side of the lamb. Combine the garlic, 2 tablespoons olive oil, and salt and pepper to taste in a small bowl. Rub the mixture on the meat.

Toss the peppers and zucchini with the remaining olive oil and season to taste with salt and pepper.

Over medium-hot coals, grill the meat and peppers about 8 minutes per side for medium rare, and the zucchini about 4 minutes per side, or until scored and tender. Watch the vegetables and remove the individual pieces when they are cooked.

Remove the meat from the grill and let it rest in a warm place for 5 minutes. Cover the vegetables with foil to keep warm.

Cut each fillet into 6 slices. Place 3 slices each in the middle of 4 dinner plates. Fan out the peppers along one side of the meat and fan out the zucchini along the other side.

Mix together the greens, tomato, scallions, and endive. Toss with ½ cup dressing and arrange the salad on each plate.

Drizzle the remaining dressing over the meat. Top the meat with the Anaheim chile.

SERVES 4

THAI LIME-MINT DRESSING

Nam pla (Thai fish sauce) is an integral part of Thai food preparation and is as commonly used in Thailand as tomato sauce is in the United States. Both fresh lemongrass and *nam pla* can be found in most Asian markets.

1 stalk lemongrass	1 jalapeño chile, seeded and minced
3 tablespoons *nam pla*	3 tablespoons fresh lime juice
2 teaspoons minced garlic	1 tablespoon honey
2 tablespoons chopped fresh mint	6 tablespoons olive oil

Remove at least 3 layers of the tough outer leaves of the lemongrass. Chop enough of the white end to measure 1 tablespoon. Mix with the *nam pla,* garlic, mint, jalapeño, lime juice, and honey. Stir in the olive oil. Let sit for 30 minutes so the flavors can blend.

MAKES ABOUT 1 CUP

PAPAS MISTO WITH RED LEAF LETTUCE AND CILANTRO SALAD

⊐IIIⅭ

The taco stands in Cabo San Lucas, Mexico, sell these potatoes, which are baked on the spot in hot coals. Carne asada is skirt steak that has been split and pounded flat. It can be found at Latin American supermarkets. If you can't find it, ask your butcher to split the steak, or do it yourself. Flank steak, turkey, or chicken are equally delicious in these potatoes.

4	huge baking potatoes, scrubbed	4	cups shredded red leaf lettuce
1	pound carne asada–style skirt steak	2	cups coarsely chopped cilantro leaves
	Olive oil		Lime Vinaigrette (recipe follows)
	Salt and freshly ground pepper	¼	cup chopped red onion
8	tablespoons unsalted butter	¼	cup chopped tomato
6	ounces Jack cheese, crumbled	1	large avocado

Preheat the oven to 450°F. Puncture the potatoes with a fork in a few places. Bake for 45 to 50 minutes, until the skins are crisp and the potatoes are soft. You can bake the potatoes in a medium-hot covered grill on the rack. Turn them once or twice while baking.

If you're preparing the meat yourself, cut it into 4- or 5-inch pieces. Split each piece as for butterflying so it is about ¼ inch thick. Lightly pound to flatten. Rub the meat with a little oil. Sprinkle with salt and pepper to taste. Grill over medium-high heat for 2 to 3 minutes per side, or just until pink when slit with a knife. Let sit a few minutes, then cut on an angle with the grain into bite-size pieces.

Split the potatoes down the center, but don't cut in two. Place 1 to 2 tablespoons of butter inside each potato and top with a little cheese. Place in a hot covered grill or a hot oven just long enough to melt the cheese, 2 to 3 minutes.

Meanwhile, toss the lettuce and cilantro with just enough Lime Vinaigrette to coat the leaves. Arrange on 4 plates.

Remove the potatoes from the grill, place on plates, and squeeze open each potato. Top with portions of the carne asada, onion, and tomato. Peel the avocado, cut into ⅛-inch pieces, and garnish the potato.

SERVES 4

LIME VINAIGRETTE

¾ cup safflower oil
¼ cup lime juice

3 garlic cloves, smashed
   Salt and freshly ground pepper

About ½ hour before serving, combine all the ingredients in a bowl. Refrigerate, covered. Remove the garlic before tossing with the greens.

MAKES 1 CUP

LAVENDER LAMB WITH WARM MUSHROOM SALAD

As the lamb cooks, the fresh herbs will begin to smoke and burn. Alternatively, you can strew the herbs on top of the glowing coals just before cooking the lamb.

1 pound boneless lamb fillet or tenderloin
   Olive oil, for rubbing
   Salt and freshly ground pepper
1 handful fresh lavender branches
1 handful fresh rosemary branches
½ cup extra-virgin olive oil

2 tablespoons lemon juice
½ pound mushrooms, cleaned and sliced
1 head butter lettuce, leaves washed, dried, and separated
   Lavender flowers

Trim the tendons and fat from the lamb. Rub with olive oil and season with salt and pepper to taste. Place the herbs on the grill rack. Place the meat on top. Grill, covered, over medium heat, turning once, 8 to 10 minutes per side for medium. Portions of the meat may be slightly charred. Let the meat rest for 10 minutes, then slice and keep warm.

In a measuring cup, combine the oil, lemon juice, and salt and pepper to taste. Pour into a medium skillet and heat until warm but not hot. Stir in the mushrooms and cook 1 minute, or just until they are warmed through. Pour them over the lettuce and quickly toss.

Arrange the salad on 2 plates. Serve with the lamb slices on the side. Garnish with lavender flowers.

SERVES 2

LAMB AND VEGETABLE KABOBS WITH GRILLED RED PEPPER SAUCE AND FENNEL SALAD

Grilling any cold meat and room-temperature vegetables on a covered grill allows them to cook together more evenly. If you wish, skewer the vegetables and meat separately and cook until both reach desired doneness.

MARINADE

4 tablespoons ground cumin
2 tablespoons sweet Hungarian paprika
2 tablespoons curry powder
1 teaspoon chili powder
   Salt and freshly ground pepper

½ cup finely chopped cilantro leaves
½ cup olive oil
¼ cup fresh lime juice
1 medium head of garlic, cloves peeled and finely chopped

---

1 boneless leg of lamb (about 4 pounds), cut into 1-inch cubes
1 large eggplant (about 2 pounds), cut into 1-inch cubes
4 small zucchini, cut into ½-inch rounds

Olive oil
Salt and freshly ground pepper
2 cups Grilled Red Pepper Sauce (page 147)
Fennel leaves
Fennel Salad (recipe follows)

Combine all the ingredients for the marinade in a large bowl. Add the lamb and toss to coat. Cover and marinate for 4 hours, or overnight in the refrigerator. Keep chilled until ready to cook.

If the vegetables have been refrigerated, bring them to room temperature before grilling. Toss the eggplant in the marinade with the lamb just before grilling. Toss the zucchini in a little oil. Sprinkle with salt and pepper to taste, then alternately thread the cold lamb, eggplant, and zucchini onto the skewers, leaving ¼ inch in between. Reserve any remaining marinade.

Grill, covered, over high or medium-high heat for 8 to 12 minutes, frequently basting with the marinade and turning to brown evenly. The lamb should be well browned on the outside and pink inside. The eggplant and zucchini should be soft. To serve, drizzle a little Grilled Red Pepper Sauce over the lamb and garnish with fennel leaves. Accompany with Fennel Salad.

SERVES 8

FENNEL SALAD

For a crunchy salad, serve immediately. If you prefer less crunch, let the fennel sit
20 minutes to absorb some of the dressing.

4 large fennel bulbs, trimmed of stalks,
   leaves reserved for garnish
½ small red onion, thinly sliced
¼ cup chopped Italian parsley leaves

Juice of 1 lemon
½ cup extra-virgin olive oil
Salt and freshly ground pepper

Slice the fennel lengthwise into paper-thin slices. In a large bowl, toss with the remaining ingredients. Adjust the salt and pepper to taste and serve immediately.

SERVES 8

LEMON LAMB KABOBS WITH TABBOULEH

For an easy summer party, accompany this dish with Moroccan Vegetable Salad (page 23) and one or two kinds of chutney.

MARINADE PASTE

½ teaspoon saffron

1 whole lemon, including rind, cut into pieces

1 small white onion, peeled and quartered

½ cup olive oil

⅓ cup chopped parsley

¼ cup chopped fresh cilantro

6 garlic cloves, peeled

1 tablespoon ground cumin

1 tablespoon paprika

1 tablespoon salt

2 teaspoons ground cinnamon

1 teaspoon freshly ground black pepper

¾ teaspoon ground coriander

¾ teaspoon turmeric

½ teaspoon cayenne pepper

---

3 pounds boneless leg of lamb, trimmed and cut into 1-inch cubes

1 large romaine lettuce, washed, dried, and leaves separated

Tabbouleh (recipe follows)

Hothouse cucumber slices

Dissolve the saffron in 2 tablespoons of water. Put all the marinade ingredients in the bowl of a food processor and process until well combined.

Place the lamb in a roasting pan or Ziploc bag and pour the marinade over. Toss to completely coat the cubes. Cover and refrigerate at least 6 hours or overnight, turning the meat 1 or 2 times. Bring to room temperature before grilling.

Thread the meat onto 12 skewers, leaving about ¼-inch space between the cubes. Grill over medium-hot coals for 8 to 10 minutes, turning frequently until browned and done to your liking.

Select 6 of the most perfect romaine leaves to use as cups. Break the remaining leaves into 3-inch pieces to be used as little scoops for the Tabbouleh. Place 2 skewers on each plate. Pile the Tabbouleh into the romaine cups, and place next to the skewers. Garnish with cucumber slices and romaine pieces.

SERVES 6

TABBOULEH

Tabbouleh is a Lebanese parsley and mint salad mixed with a small amount of cracked wheat to give it a robust and chewy texture. It's best served several hours after it's made, but it will keep overnight in the refrigerator.

½ cup fine bulgur wheat, washed and drained	3 or 4 large ripe tomatoes, peeled and finely chopped
3½ cups finely chopped Italian parsley	1 teaspoon salt
1 cup chopped fresh mint leaves	¼ teaspoon allspice
½ cup finely chopped scallions	¼ teaspoon freshly ground pepper
½ small red or Maui onion, finely chopped	Extra-virgin olive oil
¼ cup fresh lemon juice	

Combine all the ingredients except the oil in a large bowl. Mix well and adjust the salt and pepper to taste. Cover and refrigerate several hours. Just before serving, toss in at least ¼ cup olive oil or to taste.

SERVES 6

❙ ❙ ❙

PORK LOIN WITH CELERY ROOT, CORN, AND SHIITAKE SALAD

⊐ı ı ı ı⊏

Celery root has a tendency to darken, so prepare the salad just before you grill the pork or grill the pork first and keep it warm while preparing the salad.

SALAD

1 pound shiitake mushrooms, cleaned, stems removed and discarded

½ cup olive oil

3 large celery roots, peeled and julienned (6 to 7 cups)

4 cups fresh or frozen white or yellow corn

½ cup diced Marinated Sun-Dried Tomatoes (page 157)

6 tablespoons chopped Italian parsley
Salt and freshly ground pepper

---

8 slices pork loin (3½ ounces each), cut ½ inch thick, or 8 boneless pork chops
Garlic Oil (page 160)

Salt and freshly ground pepper

4 small heads lollo rossa lettuce (baby red leaf)
Chopped parsley

Slice the mushrooms into ¼-inch strips. Heat the oil in a large skillet. Sauté the celery roots and mushrooms for 5 minutes. Stir in the corn and tomatoes and cook until the corn is warmed through, 1 to 2 minutes. Stir in the parsley and season with salt and pepper to taste. Keep warm or, if you prefer, let come to room temperature.

Brush both sides of the pork with Garlic Oil and sprinkle with salt and pepper. Grill over medium-hot coals for 3 to 4 minutes per side, or until cooked through.

Separate the leaves of each head of lettuce and arrange into a cup shape on one side of each plate. Fill the lettuce with the corn salad and sprinkle with a little chopped parsley. Place the pork slices next to the salad and serve.

SERVES 4

Pork Loin with Celery Root, Corn, and Shiitake Salad

CHINESE ORANGE CARNITAS

⊐ ⅼ ⅼ ⅼ ⊏

The meat, noodles, and salad can be rolled in Chinese crepes or soft flour tortillas to be eaten like a Chinese burrito.

MARINADE

½ cup soy sauce

2 teaspoons five-spice powder

½ cup sugar

3 tablespoons sake

2 tablespoons rice vinegar

1 tablespoon peanut oil

1 tablespoon dark sesame oil

2 tablespoons Hoisin sauce

---

2 pounds boneless pork loin, in 1-inch cubes

DRESSING

2 cups mandarin or regular orange juice

¼ cup rice vinegar

½ cup peanut oil

2 tablespoons soy sauce

2 sprigs tarragon

1 cup Sweet Ginger and Garlic Dressing (page 51)

2 cups cellophane noodles

2 cups tatsoi leaves or baby bok choy

2 cups torn arugula

2 cups torn sorrel

2 cups watercress

2 papayas, peeled, seeded, and cubed

1 cup toasted pine nuts

Mix marinade ingredients together in a bowl. Pour into a shallow pan or Ziploc bag. Add the meat and coat well. Refrigerate at least 6 hours.

For the dressing, combine the orange juice, vinegar, oil, soy sauce, and tarragon in a medium saucepan. Cook over medium heat until very syrupy or reduced to about ¾ to ½ cup. Mix with ½ cup Sweet Ginger and Garlic Dressing. Set aside.

Cook the noodles according to package directions. Drain and mix with the remaining Sweet Ginger and Garlic dressing. Set aside.

Have 8 stainless steel or bamboo skewers ready. If using bamboo skewers, remember to soak them in water for 15 to 20 minutes before threading. Thread the pork cubes on the skewers about ¼ inch apart and grill over medium-high heat 15 to 20 minutes, basting as necessary and turning frequently, until the pork is well browned. Remove from skewers, cover, and keep warm. Toss the greens, papayas, and pine nuts with enough orange dressing to coat lightly.

Arrange ½ cup noodles each on 4 plates. Top with the greens and pork.

SERVES 4

BARBECUED PORK TENDERLOIN SALAD

Pork tenderloins cook very quickly and are very tender. Accompany this dish with Grilled New Potato and Asparagus Salad (page 28), corn on the cob, or baked potatoes.

1 pork tenderloin, ¾ to 1 pound, trimmed
   of fat
   Barbecue Sauce (page 157)
   Olive oil
2 tablespoons red wine vinegar
1 garlic clove, smashed
1 teaspoon Dijon mustard

Salt and freshly ground pepper
1 large red onion, cut into ½-inch-thick
   slices
6 ounces mixed field greens
5 yellow pear tomatoes, halved
5 red cherry tomatoes, halved

Place the pork in a shallow nonreactive dish. Pour over enough Barbecue Sauce to coat the pork liberally. Wrap in plastic and marinate overnight in the refrigerator.

For the dressing, mix 6 tablespoons olive oil with the vinegar, garlic, and mustard in a small bowl. Add salt and pepper to taste. Set aside.

Bring the pork to room temperature. Brush with a little more Barbecue Sauce, using just enough to coat.

Grill the meat over hot coals. Cook, turning and brushing several times with Barbecue Sauce, for 18 to 25 minutes, or until a meat thermometer inserted in the thickest part of the meat reads 150°F. to 155°F. and the meat is no longer pink inside. Let the meat rest for 10 minutes.

Meanwhile, brush the onion slices with a little olive oil. Grill over medium-hot coals, 3 to 4 minutes per side, until browned and soft.

Remove the garlic from the dressing and toss with the greens. Arrange on 2 plates.

Slice the pork into thin slices and layer on top of the greens. Strew the tomatoes and onions on top of the greens and pork. Serve with extra Barbecue Sauce.

SERVES 2

GORGONZOLA CHEESEBURGER ON GARLIC-ROSEMARY FOCACCIA

Freshly ground chuck makes a terrific, juicy burger because of its fat-to-lean ratio (about 15 percent fat). If using a leaner cut of meat, such as ground round or sirloin, it's best to cook the burgers to either rare or medium rare to avoid dryness.

1½ pounds ground chuck
8 slices Rosemary-Garlic Focaccia (page 138)
4 romaine or iceberg lettuce leaves

4 thin slices red onion, Vidalia, or Maui
4 Italian plum (Roma) tomatoes, sliced
¼ pound gorgonzola cheese, crumbled

Gently form 4 patties, about 1 inch thick, by pressing the meat together just until the burgers hold together, being careful not to overpack them. Cook burgers on an open grill over medium-hot coals 4 to 6 minutes per side for rare to medium-rare, turning once. Meanwhile, grill the focaccia just to warm it through.

Place a lettuce leaf, burger, onion slice, tomato slice, and some gorgonzola between 2 slices of the focaccia for each serving and serve.

SERVES 4

TERIYAKI RIB EYE STEAK DIP

Gerri's brother Paul Gilliland created this sandwich. You can purchase thinly sliced beef in a Japanese market. If you're cutting the steak at home, partially freeze the meat before slicing.

TERIYAKI SAUCE

1 cup soy sauce	2 garlic cloves, crushed
1 cup mirin (Japanese rice wine) or sake	1 tablespoon chopped fresh ginger
1 cup sugar	

1½ pounds rib eye steak, thinly sliced	1 pound mushrooms, cleaned and thinly sliced
4 tablespoons unsalted butter	6 French or kaiser rolls, split

Combine the sauce ingredients in a medium saucepan. Cook 10 minutes over medium heat and set aside.

Quickly grill the meat over hot coals on a lightly oiled grill, about 1 minute per side. Because it is so thinly sliced, the meat might stick to the grill as it cooks. Use a metal scraper or spatula to remove it from the grill. Place on a platter and pour ½ cup teriyaki sauce over the meat.

Melt the butter in a large sauté pan. Add the mushrooms and sauté over high heat until soft and slightly golden, 5 to 10 minutes.

Split the rolls in half and grill, cut side down, just until lightly toasted, 1 to 2 minutes. Place equal portions of meat and mushrooms on the rolls, then close sandwiches. Serve extra sauce separately on the side for dipping.

SERVES 6

Gorgonzola Cheeseburger on Garlic-Rosemary Focaccia

CARNE ASADA TORTA

⊐ιιιι⊏

Skirt steak makes the best carne asada, but any steak such as tenderloin, sirloin, or even filet mignon can be used. See page 78 for directions on how to cut carne asada.

1½ pounds skirt steak, trimmed of fat	3 tablespoons Mayonnaise (page 159)
¼ cup olive oil	1 avocado, sliced
4 garlic cloves, peeled and finely chopped	3 scallions, root end trimmed and chopped
½ teaspoon ground cumin	1½ cups shredded iceberg or romaine lettuce
Freshly ground pepper	Chiles in Orange Escabèche (page 153)
Salt	or Grilled Onion and Garlic Relish
Juice of 1 lime	(page 150)
3 French or kaiser rolls	
¾ cup Refried Black Beans (recipe follows or see Duck Tacos, page 58)	

Place the meat in a Ziploc bag or glass dish. In a measuring cup, combine the olive oil, garlic, cumin, and freshly ground pepper to taste. Pour over the meat to completely cover. Cover and marinate overnight in the refrigerator.

Before cooking, bring the meat to room temperature. Sprinkle with salt to taste. Grill over high heat 2 to 3 minutes per side for medium rare, or to desired doneness. Sprinkle with lime juice.

Slice the rolls three-quarters of the way through. Spread one side of each roll with 2 to 3 tablespoons Refried Black Beans and spread the other side with Mayonnaise.

Fill the rolls with the avocado slices, scallions, lettuce, and meat. Serve immediately, garnished with Chiles in Orange Escabèche or Grilled Onion and Garlic Relish.

MAKES 3 SANDWICHES

REFRIED BLACK BEANS

We find the Goya brand of black beans, available in some supermarkets, natural foods stores, and Latin American markets, superior to most other brands.

1 to 2 tablespoons peanut oil
   3 cups cooked or canned black beans, drained and rinsed
  ¼ small white onion, diced
   1 jalapeño chile, sliced, with seeds intact

1 small tomato, diced
½ teaspoon salt
½ teaspoon freshly ground pepper
⅓ cup packed chopped cilantro leaves

Heat the oil in a medium frying pan. Add the beans, onion, jalapeño, tomato, salt, and pepper. Cook over high heat, mashing the beans with the back of a spoon as the beans fry. After 5 minutes, add the cilantro. Cook about 5 more minutes, or until the beans are dry. Set aside and keep warm.

MAKES ABOUT 2 CUPS

▮ ▮ ▮

SAUSAGE AND POLENTA SANDWICH WITH DRIED AND FRESH TOMATO-HERB RELISH

⊐ııııⵊ

If you prefer, precook the sausages by simmering them in water for 20 minutes. Either split them down the center after poaching or grill whole with the polenta. The polenta is best prepared the day before grilling. Accompany with mixed greens tossed with a little oil and vinegar.

Olive oil

POLENTA

3½ cups chicken stock

1¼ cups polenta or coarse cornmeal

2 tablespoons unsalted butter

SALSA

¾ pound ripe Italian plum tomatoes, seeded, cut into ¼-inch dice

⅓ cup chopped Marinated Sun-Dried Tomatoes [page 157]

⅓ cup chopped fresh basil leaves

¼ cup diced Maui onion

2 teaspoons minced fresh sage

2 garlic cloves, minced

1 tablespoon sun-dried tomato oil, reserved from the Marinated Sun-Dried Tomatoes

Freshly ground pepper

---

8 hot Italian sausages

Generously oil an 8-inch square Pyrex pan. Set aside.

To make the polenta, bring the chicken stock to a boil, then pour in the polenta in a slow stream, stirring constantly with a whisk until all the liquid is absorbed. Immediately lower the heat and using a wooden spoon, stir continuously until the mixture is thick and begins to pull away from the sides of the pan, 15 to 20 minutes. Stir in the butter and remove from heat.

Spread the polenta into the prepared pan, evenly smoothing the surface with a rubber spatula dipped in cold water. Lightly brush with oil. Let cool, then cover. Refrigerate for at least 8 hours or overnight.

About 1 hour before serving, combine the salsa ingredients. Cover and set aside.

Sausage and Polenta Sandwich with Dried and Fresh Tomato-Herb Relish

Place the sausages on an oiled grill, cover, and cook over medium-hot coals, turning frequently to brown evenly, 10 to 12 minutes, or until the juices run clear when poked with a sharp knife. (A spray bottle filled with water should be kept near the grill in case of flare-ups from dripping fat.) Remove the sausages from the grill and keep warm.

Invert the cold polenta onto a cutting board. Cut into quarters, then cut each quarter into 2 triangles. Brush each side with oil and grill on an oiled grill over medium-hot coals, about 4 minutes per side, until heated through, lightly browned, and crusty.

Place 2 triangles of polenta and 2 sausages on each plate. Spoon a little salsa over the sausages and serve immediately, with extra salsa on the side.

SERVES 4

BALSAMIC-ROSEMARY LAMB
SANDWICH WITH RED ONION CONFIT

A grilled butterflied leg of lamb will have various degrees of doneness—from medium rare to well—because of the uneven thickness of the meat. This sandwich is good with a green salad and french fries.

1   (5- to 6-pound) leg of lamb, boned and
    butterflied, trimmed of all fat

MARINADE

4½	tablespoons balsamic vinegar	6	garlic cloves, finely chopped
¼	cup extra-virgin olive oil	½	cup chopped fresh basil leaves
3	tablespoons light soy sauce	¼	cup chopped fresh rosemary leaves
2	tablespoons lemon juice	¼	teaspoon freshly ground pepper
4	shallots, finely chopped		

16	thick slices sourdough or any bread yielding large slices	½	cup Pesto Mayonnaise (page 159)
8	garlic cloves, peeled and halved Olive oil Salt and freshly ground pepper	3	cups thinly sliced or shredded romaine lettuce leaves
		4	Italian plum (Roma) tomatoes, sliced Red Onion Confit (page 149)

Place the lamb in a roasting pan or Ziploc bag. Combine the marinade ingredients in a measuring cup and pour over the lamb to coat completely. Cover and let sit 1 hour at room temperature, or refrigerate at least 6 hours. Bring the lamb to room temperature before cooking. Grill over medium-hot coals on an oiled grill 12 to 20 minutes per side. A meat thermometer should read 140° F. (medium rare) when inserted into the thickest part of the lamb. When done, remove to a cutting board and let rest for 10 to 15 minutes before slicing thinly.

Meanwhile, rub both sides of the bread with the garlic and brush with a little olive oil. Season with salt and pepper. Grill bread on both sides until light golden brown, 1 to 2 minutes. Spread one side of each slice with Pesto Mayonnaise. Sprinkle half the slices with greens and tomatoes, and top with the lamb. Dot with Red Onion Confit, close the sandwiches, slice in half diagonally, and serve immediately.

MAKES 8 HUGE SANDWICHES

Omit the Pesto Mayonnaise and Red Onion Confit. Replace 1 cup shredded lettuce with 1 cup shredded fresh basil leaves. Toss basil and lettuce together. Grill 16 slices of Basil Bread (page 136) as above. Cut the tomatoes in half. Rub the tomatoes, cut side down, over all the slices of grilled bread so the juices sink into the bread. Discard the tomatoes. Layer on the hot lamb slices, lettuce, and basil. Garnish with Grilled Onion and Garlic Relish (page 150).

TENDERLOIN OF BEEF AND HUMMUS SANDWICH

Grilled tenderloin will be well done on the ends and medium to medium rare in the center, so everyone can have his or her preferred cut of meat.

1½ pounds tenderloin, trimmed of fat	½ pound good-quality blue cheese
2 to 3 tablespoons olive oil	1½ ounces (about 2 cups) mixed baby greens
Salt and freshly cracked or ground pepper	4 medium ripe Italian plum (Roma) tomatoes, thinly sliced
4 (6-inch) French rolls, poppyseed kaiser rolls, or pita bread	1 small Maui or red onion, thinly sliced
½ cup Hummus (page 143)	

Rub the tenderloin with 1 tablespoon oil and salt and pepper to taste. Grill 4 to 6 inches above hot coals for 15 minutes on one side. Turn and grill an additional 15 to 20 minutes. Let meat rest 10 minutes before thinly slicing.

Cut the rolls in half and brush with the remaining olive oil. Grill, cut side down, just until golden, 1 or 2 minutes. Spread each piece with about 2 tablespoons Hummus. Crumble the blue cheese and place on the top halves of the rolls, lightly pressing it into the Hummus.

Layer the greens, tomatoes, meat, and onions on the bottom half of each roll. Cover with the top half, securing with toothpicks if necessary.

SERVES 4

S E A F O O D

S A L A D S

Pink Trout with Cucumber-Chive Salad

Salmon Wrapped in Leeks with Warm Red Bell Pepper Puree

Salmon with Arugula-Watercress Salad and Tomato Vinaigrette

Norwegian Salmon on Fennel with Green Sauce

Crunchy Mustard Sea Bass with Arugula and Pink Lentil Salad

Grilled Tuna Salade Niçoise

Rare Tuna Salad with Avocado and Daikon Sprouts

Leek and Basil–Stuffed Swordfish with Chopped Confetti Salad

Swordfish on Escarole with Tomato-Basil Salad

Halibut Steaks with Papaya Salsa

Catfish on Asian Greens

Almond-Coated Mahimahi with Mango Vinaigrette and Grilled Plantains

Scallop Salad with Avocado, White Corn, and Maui Onions

Grilled Shrimps with Chipotle-Orange Sauce and Tomatillo Salsa

Lula Bertran's Grilled Shrimps and Scallops with Mango Mayonnaise and Fried Cilantro

Lobster with Four-Grain Salad

Tom Mitchell's Lime Shrimps with Black Bean Vinaigrette

Sea Scallops with Bell Pepper Vinaigrette

Grilled Shrimps, Jack Cheese, and Avocado Tostada

S A N D W I C H E S

Seafood Sausages on Catalan Tomato Bread with Fava Bean Salad

Calamari Steak and Coleslaw Sandwich

Grilled Salmon BLT

Lobster and Mozzarella Melt

M ost seafood lovers will agree that one of the best ways to enjoy any type of fish or shellfish—from whole fish to steaks, fillets, or even kabobs—is to cook it on the grill. The high heat quickly sears the sweet flesh, thereby sealing in the juices and keeping the fish moist.

Before cooking, always lightly brush the fish on both sides with oil, then place it on a clean, lightly oiled grill 4 to 6 inches above the heat. (If using charcoal, the coals should be covered in a light gray ash.) You can cook delicate or small portions of fish on a lightly oiled porcelain-coated grilling rack or in a stainless steel hinged basket specifically designed for this purpose.

Measure fish at its thickest part, then cook, turning once, 6 to 12 minutes per inch, or until firm, and no longer translucent. Contrary to popular thought, cooked fish that easily flakes with a fork is overcooked. Fish, like meat, will continue to cook once it has been removed from the heat, so it is best to undercook fish slightly to prevent dryness.

In many of the following recipes, we've recommended other varieties of fish that can be substituted, but these are strictly personal preferences. Seafood is very adaptable, so feel free to experiment by trying your own favorite fish.

PRECEDING SPREAD: *Lobster with Four-Grain Salad (page 122)*

PINK TROUT WITH
CUCUMBER-CHIVE SALAD

⊐ııııⅭ

Perfect for a special luncheon or dinner party, this dish is also delicious using regular trout, Coho salmon, or salmon trout for pink trout.

SALAD

1 English or hothouse cucumber, peeled and thinly sliced	1 tablespoon champagne vinegar
Kosher salt	¾ cup heavy cream
2 teaspoons sugar	3 tablespoons extra-virgin olive oil
	Salt and freshly ground pepper

4 pink trout, heads removed, boned and split	¼ cup chopped chives
Olive oil	4 Boston or Bibb lettuce leaves, cleaned and dried
Salt and freshly ground pepper	8 whole chive spears

Place the cucumber slices in a colander. Sprinkle with a little salt and let drain for 30 minutes. Rinse the cucumbers to remove excess salt. Drain well and pat dry. Refrigerate until ready to serve.

Meanwhile, in a small bowl, mix the sugar with the vinegar, then slowly whisk in the cream to increase the volume. Whisk in the extra-virgin olive oil until well combined and season with salt and pepper to taste. Chill until ready to serve.

Rub both sides of the trout with oil and season with salt and pepper. Grill, flesh side down, on a lightly oiled grill over hot coals for 2 to 3 minutes, then rotate a half turn to create crisscross grill marks. Grill 2 minutes more, then turn the fish over. Grill an additional 3½ to 4 minutes, or until the flesh is firm and opaque. Cover and keep warm.

Mix the cucumbers and dressing together. Sprinkle with chopped chives and toss lightly. Place a lettuce leaf on each plate and add the cucumber salad. Garnish with a crisscross of whole chives. Place the fish on the plates and serve immediately.

SERVES 4

SALMON WRAPPED IN LEEKS WITH WARM RED BELL PEPPER PUREE

⊐ I I I I ⊏

Buy the fattest leeks you can find. The wider the leek, the easier it will be to wrap the salmon. The salmon should be moist inside and slightly undercooked.

4 large leeks, root end trimmed	1 tablespoon fresh lime juice
4 (8-ounce) salmon fillets, bones removed	Salt and freshly ground pepper
4 large red bell peppers	Olive oil
⅔ cup extra-virgin olive oil	Chervil

Cut off and discard the green end of the leeks, leaving about 8 inches of white. Clean thoroughly. Fill with water a pan large enough to accommodate the length of the leeks. Bring to a boil. Place the leeks in the water, lower the heat, and simmer for 8 to 12 minutes, or until soft. Drain, cool, and split the leeks lengthwise only to the center of the stalk so that the leeks can be opened flat and the stalk can be separated.

For each piece of salmon, overlap 2 of the largest and prettiest pieces of stalk, smooth (interior) side up, to form an oblong large enough to wrap completely around the salmon. Place the salmon, boned side down, in the middle of the leek pieces. Wrap each salmon fillet in the leek by folding each end of the leek up and over the entire salmon fillet, so that no part of the fish is exposed and the leek ends meet in the center of the package. The seams of the leek package should look like the back of an envelope. Place the packets on a plate, seam side down, and refrigerate until ready to cook. Slice the interiors of the remaining cooked leeks and reserve for garnish.

Grill the peppers over very hot coals or a gas flame until blackened, about 10 minutes. Place in a paper or plastic bag and steam for 10 to 15 minutes. Peel off the charred skin with your fingers or a sharp paring knife. Remove the stems and seeds and cut the peppers in half. (Peppers can be prepared up to a week in advance and stored in a jar filled with oil to cover until ready to use.)

Place the peppers in a food processor and process to a thick puree. Scrape into a saucepan. Add the extra-virgin olive oil, lime juice, and salt and pepper to taste. Heat the sauce and keep warm.

Remove the salmon from the refrigerator about 15 minutes before grilling. Generously brush all over with olive oil. Grill, seam side up first, over hot coals, 4 to 5 minutes per side, carefully turning.

Place each salmon-leek package, folded side down, on 4 plates. Spoon the sauce around the salmon and garnish with the remaining leeks and chervil.

SERVES 4

SALMON WITH ARUGULA-WATERCRESS SALAD AND TOMATO VINAIGRETTE

This dish is excellent made with any fatty fish such as swordfish, mahimahi, or yellowtail. Cooking the fillets with the skin on helps keep the fish in one piece while turning, as well as making the skin easier to remove once the fish is cooked.

VINAIGRETTE

10 extra large garlic cloves, unpeeled	¼ cup olive oil
2 pounds ripe Italian plum (Roma) tomatoes, peeled, seeded, and diced	Juice of 1 lime (about 2 tablespoons)
	1 teaspoon salt
3 sprigs fresh rosemary, coarsely chopped	1 teaspoon freshly ground pepper

SALAD

2 cups chopped arugula	Olive oil
2 cups watercress leaves	Salt and freshly ground pepper
Balsamic vinegar	

4 (6-ounce) salmon fillets	Salt and freshly ground pepper
Olive oil	Rosemary sprigs

Put the garlic in a small pan of cold water. Bring to a boil and simmer 1 minute. Discard the water and repeat the procedure 4 times. (The repeated boiling in fresh water refreshes the garlic and removes all bitterness.) Poach the garlic until al dente, drain, and refresh in ice water. Peel and cut into slivers.

Mix together the garlic, tomatoes, rosemary, olive oil, lime juice, salt, and pepper. Set aside.

Mix the arugula and watercress with a little balsamic vinegar and olive oil to coat lightly. Season with salt and pepper to taste.

Brush the salmon fillets with a little oil and season with salt and pepper. Grill the salmon over hot coals for 4 to 5 minutes per side, until translucent in the center for medium rare.

Place each salmon fillet on a dinner plate. Top one end of the fish with the vinaigrette. Place the arugula mixture alongside the fish. Garnish with rosemary.

SERVES 4

NORWEGIAN SALMON ON FENNEL WITH GREEN SAUCE

You need only a small amount of this delicate green sauce, which is similar to an herb mayonnaise.

GREEN SAUCE

2 tablespoons capers	2 large hard-cooked egg yolks
1 tablespoon parsley leaves	1 large raw egg yolk
1 whole shallot	1 cup extra-virgin olive oil
2 garlic cloves	Juice of 1 lemon
2 anchovies, rinsed and patted dry	White pepper

2 large whole fennel bulbs with leaves	4 (6-ounce) Norwegian salmon fillets
Olive oil	Salt and freshly ground pepper

In a food processor or blender, chop the capers, parsley, shallot, garlic, and anchovies. With the motor running, add the cooked and raw egg yolks, then slowly pour in the oil. Add the lemon juice. Add pepper to taste. Cover and chill until ready to use. The sauce will keep for 3 to 4 days in the refrigerator. Bring to room temperature before using.

Remove the stalks and leaves from the fennel and reserve. Cut the bulbs into quarters and brush with oil.

Brush the salmon with a little oil and season with salt and pepper. Place the fennel stalks on an oiled grill and top with the salmon. Cook the fish over hot coals, turning once, 5 to 6 minutes per side. The fennel will char very quickly. Discard fennel when turning fish. Remove the fish and keep warm if necessary.

Place the fennel bulbs on the grill, cut side down, and grill 5 to 10 minutes, until warmed and scored, turning to cook all sides. If the fennel begins to burn, move it away from the coals to a cooler part of the grill.

Transfer the fennel bulbs and fish to serving plates. Top the fish with a dollop of green sauce. Garnish with the reserved fennel leaves.

SERVES 4

Crunchy Mustard Sea Bass with Arugula and Pink Lentil Salad

CRUNCHY MUSTARD SEA BASS WITH ARUGULA AND PINK LENTIL SALAD

⊐ııııⅭ

Lentils are not only good for you; they're delicious. Pink lentils are smaller than the brown ones and cook quickly. You can find them in health food stores and Middle Eastern and Indian markets.

2 (6- to 8-ounce) sea bass fillets	¼ cup black mustard seeds
Olive oil	Arugula and Pink Lentil Salad (recipe
Salt and freshly ground pepper	follows)

Rub the fish with olive oil. Sprinkle with salt and pepper, then lightly pat the rounded side of the fish with mustard seeds. Grill over hot coals on an oiled grill, or a grill basket, seed side down first, about 7 minutes. Turn and grill an additional 8 minutes, until the flesh is firm and opaque. Serve with lentil salad.

SERVES 2

ARUGULA AND PINK LENTIL SALAD

½ cup pink lentils, rinsed in cold water	Salt and freshly ground pepper
1 garlic clove	1 cup finely chopped red onion
1 bay leaf	1 cup baby arugula
3 tablespoons extra-virgin olive oil	¼ cup chopped Italian parsley
1 tablespoon red wine vinegar	2 tomatoes, cut into wedges
¼ teaspoon ground cumin	

Place the lentils in a medium pan with the garlic and bay leaf and cover with 1½ cups cold water. Bring to a boil, lower the heat, and simmer for 5 to 8 minutes, or until soft. Do not overcook, or the lentils will be mushy. Drain and remove the garlic and bay leaf. Spread the lentils on a cookie sheet to cool.

Combine the oil, vinegar, cumin, salt, and pepper in a small cup.

Mix the lentils, onion, arugula, and parsley together in a bowl. Toss with the dressing. Garnish with tomato wedges.

SERVES 2

GRILLED TUNA SALADE NIÇOISE

⊐ιιιι⊏

The basic ingredients of a Niçoise-style dish are tomatoes, black olives, garlic, and anchovies. Add to this a little tuna, red peppers, and hard-cooked eggs, and *voila!* Purists will say that a proper Niçoise salad never contains cooked vegetables, but we've taken the liberty of steaming the beans and grilling the red potatoes. Whatever the variation, this simple salad needs only crusty bread and sweet butter plus a bottle of white or rosé wine to make an exceptional meal.

2 red peppers, halved lengthwise and seeded

12 small new potatoes, scrubbed and halved

Olive oil

½ pound green beans, trimmed to about 3 inches in length

1 cup French Vinaigrette (recipe follows)

4 (6-ounce) tuna steaks

12 ounces mesclun or field mix (such as arugula, *frisée,* mâche, watercress, chard, and baby dandelion greens)

8 red cherry tomatoes, halved

8 yellow cherry tomatoes, halved

24 Niçoise olives or any oil-cured Mediterranean black olives

4 hard-cooked eggs, quartered

8 anchovy fillets, washed, patted dry, and halved lengthwise

Grill the peppers over very hot coals or a gas flame until blackened, about 10 minutes. Place in a paper or plastic bag and steam for 10 to 15 minutes. Peel off the charred skin with your fingers or a sharp paring knife. Cut the peppers into ½-inch strips. Set aside.

Toss the potatoes in just enough oil to coat. Place on an oiled grill but not directly over the hottest coals, and cook, covered, over medium-hot heat for 10 to 15 minutes, or until lightly browned and tender when pierced. Turn several times with a spatula to insure even cooking. Remove from the grill.

Meanwhile, place the beans in a steamer over boiling water, cover, and steam for 5 to 6 minutes, until bright green and still crunchy. Remove from the heat immediately. Set aside.

While still warm, place the potatoes in a bowl and toss with just enough French Vinaigrette to coat. In a separate bowl, toss the warm green beans with just enough vinaigrette to coat.

Brush the tuna with a little vinaigrette and grill over very hot coals, about 4 to

5 minutes for rare or 7½ minutes for medium, turning once. Remove from the grill and set aside while composing the salad.

Place the mesclun in a large salad bowl. Toss with a little vinaigrette. Arrange the vegetables, olives, eggs, and anchovies around the lettuce. Drizzle with more vinaigrette to flavor. Place the tuna in the center and serve with any leftover dressing.

SERVES 4

FRENCH VINAIGRETTE

3½	tablespoons red wine vinegar		¼	teaspoon freshly ground pepper, or to taste
1	teaspoon salt			Pinch of sugar
⅔ to 1	cup extra-virgin olive oil		½	teaspoon grainy mustard
2	garlic cloves, finely minced			

Place the vinegar and salt in a small bowl and beat with a fork. Whisk in the olive oil, garlic, pepper, and sugar. Stir in the mustard. Adjust the seasonings.

MAKES ABOUT 1 CUP

Note: If there is any leftover salad, make a *pan bagnat,* a wonderful, messy salad sandwich popular in Nice for which there really is no recipe. Reserve any olives to serve on the side. Split a baguette or large country loaf in half, then remove and discard just enough bread from the center of the bottom half to accommodate the salad, including sliced leftover tuna if you wish. Cover with the top portion of bread, wrap in plastic wrap, and weight down in the refrigerator for at least 2 hours or overnight. (If the baguette is too long for the refrigerator, cut it in half before wrapping.) Slice into portions and serve.

FOLLOWING PAGE: *Grilled Tuna Salade Niçoise (opposite)*

RARE TUNA SALAD WITH AVOCADO AND DAIKON SPROUTS

This tuna must be served rare. Cooking it cold allows more control over doneness.

1 medium carrot
1 daikon (Japanese radish)
12 ounces cold tuna steak, cut into 12 thin slices
½ cup extra-virgin olive oil
¼ cup freshly squeezed lime juice
1 tablespoon plus 1 teaspoon grainy mustard
1 teaspoon wasabi (Japanese horseradish)

Salt and freshly ground pepper to taste
1 hothouse cucumber, peeled
1 ripe avocado
12 ounces mixed baby greens (such as arugula and baby red oak leaf)
8 edible flowers, such as pansies or nasturtiums
Daikon sprouts

With a potato peeler, peel the carrot and daikon, then peel 20 thin carrot strips and 20 thin daikon strips. Place the strips in ice water and refrigerate.

Arrange the tuna slices in a shallow, nonreactive pan or in a Ziploc bag. In a measuring cup, mix together the olive oil, lime juice, mustard, wasabi, and salt and pepper. Pour half of the mixture over the fish and reserve the rest. Cover the fish and refrigerate no more than 30 minutes or the marinade will begin to cook the fish like seviche.

Remove the tuna and vegetables from the refrigerator. Place the tuna on an oiled grill and quickly grill over very hot coals, no more than 2 to 3 minutes, turning once, just until rare.

Drain the carrot and daikon strips and pat dry with paper towels. Peel 20 thin strips of cucumber. Peel the avocado and cut in half lengthwise. Cut each half into 8 slices.

Place a large handful of greens in the center of 4 individual plates. Cover with 3 slices of tuna. Arrange piles of carrot, daikon, and cucumber strips around the greens. Fan out 4 avocado slices on each plate and decorate with edible flowers and daikon sprouts. Drizzle 1 tablespoon of the remaining marinade over the fish and greens. Sprinkle with a twist of black pepper.

SERVES 4

LEEK AND BASIL—STUFFED SWORDFISH WITH CHOPPED CONFETTI SALAD

This colorful dish is filled with the flavors of the Mediterranean.

1 small leek, trimmed, cleaned, and sliced
  Olive oil
  Salt and freshly ground pepper
2 (7-ounce) swordfish steaks, about ½ to ¾ inch thick

2 ounces (½ cup) grated mozzarella cheese
2 tablespoons chopped basil
  Chopped Confetti Salad (recipe follows)

Sauté the leek in 1½ tablespoons olive oil over medium heat. Season with salt and pepper to taste. Cool to room temperature.

Trim the skin from the edge of the fish. To make a pocket on the trimmed side, hold the fish flat with the palm of your hand on a cutting surface. Using the point of a sharp knife, insert it midway between the thickness of the fish and gently work the knife horizontally about halfway to two-thirds through the length of the steak. Leave about ½ inch on the sides uncut. Toss the mozzarella, basil, and leek together and gently stuff into the fish.

Brush the fish with a little oil, sprinkle with salt and pepper, and place on an oiled grill. Cook over medium-hot coals in a covered grill for 2 minutes. Rotate the fish to make scoring marks and cook for 2 minutes. Turn the fish over and grill, covered, for an additional 4 to 5 minutes.

Serve with the Chopped Confetti Salad.

SERVES 2

Stuffing Variation: Spinach and Wild Mushroom Stuffing

1 cup washed and dried julienned spinach leaves	**½** teaspoon chopped garlic
⅓ pound wild mushrooms, cleaned and coarsely chopped	Olive oil
	Salt
	Pinch of red pepper flakes

Sauté the ingredients in a little oil. Season with salt and pepper flakes to taste. Remove from the heat and cool to room temperature before stuffing, then proceed as above.

SERVES 2

CHOPPED CONFETTI SALAD

You can chop all the vegetables except the tomatoes the day before and store them in an airtight container. Just before serving, add the tomatoes and toss with the dressing.

6 tablespoons extra-virgin olive oil	**1** small zucchini, chopped
2½ tablespoons balsamic vinegar or lemon juice	**½** English cucumber, unpeeled and chopped
1 large garlic clove, minced	**1** small red bell pepper, stemmed, seeded, white pith removed, and diced
Salt and freshly ground pepper	
1 head radicchio, chopped	**1** small yellow bell pepper, stemmed, seeded, white pith removed, and diced
1 whole Belgian endive, chopped	
1 cup coarsely chopped arugula	**2** Italian plum (Roma) tomatoes, chopped

In a small bowl, whisk together the oil, vinegar, garlic, and salt and pepper to taste. Combine the vegetables and toss with enough dressing to moisten. Adjust the seasonings. Serve immediately.

SERVES 2

SWORDFISH ON ESCAROLE WITH TOMATO-BASIL SALAD

⊐ ||||⊏

Swordfish, like tuna, is a meaty fish that is best grilled or broiled.

TOMATO-BASIL SALAD

4 ripe tomatoes
½ cup extra-virgin olive oil
2 tablespoons sherry wine vinegar
1 shallot, peeled and chopped
1 bunch basil, chopped (about ¾ cup)

1 bunch chives, minced (about ½ cup)
½ teaspoon salt, or to taste
¼ teaspoon freshly ground pepper, or to taste

VINAIGRETTE FOR THE ESCAROLE

2 tablespoons red wine vinegar
1 small garlic clove, crushed

6 tablespoons extra-virgin olive oil
   Salt and freshly ground pepper to taste

---

4 (8-ounce) swordfish steaks, ¾ to 1 inch thick
   Olive oil

1 bunch escarole, washed, dried, and finely shredded

Make a small X on the bottom of each tomato with a sharp knife. Plunge them one at a time into a pot of boiling water for 30 seconds. Peel, seed, and chop.

Combine all the ingredients for the Tomato-Basil Salad in a nonreactive bowl. Refrigerate until ready to use.

Combine all the vinaigrette ingredients in a small bowl or measuring cup. Refrigerate until ready to use.

Brush the swordfish with a little oil. Sprinkle with a little salt and pepper. Place the fish on the grill over hot coals. Rotate the fish to crosshatch after 1 minute. Grill for 3 to 4 minutes per side, turning once. Cover to keep warm.

Toss the escarole with the vinaigrette, mixing well. Place the escarole on individual plates and top with the swordfish set at an angle. Spoon 2 tablespoons Tomato-Basil Salad across half of each fish. Serve the remaining salad on the side.

SERVES 4

Leek and Basil–Stuffed Swordfish with Chopped Confetti Salad (page 110)

HALIBUT STEAKS WITH PAPAYA SALSA

Halibut is a sweet, firm-textured, very lean fish. It will easily dry out if overcooked, so brush it with a little extra oil while grilling. Accompany this dish with small bowls of black beans and rice.

12 medium to large scallions	Juice of 1 lime
Olive oil	½ cup chopped cilantro
Juice of 1 lemon	Salt and freshly ground pepper
1 ripe papaya, peeled and seeded	4 (6- to 7-ounce) halibut steaks, about 1
1 jalapeño chile, seeded and diced	inch thick
¼ small red onion, diced	Fresh chervil or cilantro sprigs

Trim the root ends and 2 inches of the green tops of the scallions. In a nonreactive bowl, mix together 3 tablespoons olive oil and lemon juice. Add the scallions and marinate for 20 minutes.

Meanwhile, cut the papaya into ½-inch cubes. Place in a small, nonreactive bowl and mix in the jalapeños, onion, lime juice, and cilantro. Season with salt and pepper to taste.

Rub the halibut with oil and sprinkle with a little salt and pepper. Place the halibut and scallions over hot coals. Cook the halibut, 10 to 12 minutes, turning once, until the fish is firm and opaque, and the scallions, 5 to 10 minutes, or until soft, turning often to evenly brown. Arrange halibut and scallions on individual plates. Top one end of the fish with the papaya salsa and garnish with chervil sprigs.

SERVES 4

CATFISH ON ASIAN GREENS

⊐ ı ı ı ı ⊏

This is a light dish that's easily prepared in less than 30 minutes.

4 ounces Asian field greens (such as baby spinach, bok choy, red mustard, mizuna, and tatsoi)
2 (6-ounce) catfish fillets
Peanut oil
Salt and freshly ground pepper
1 tablespoon unsalted butter

¼ cup rice vinegar
¼ cup mirin or sake
2 tablespoons light soy sauce
½ cup minced scallions, including green part
1 tablespoon black sesame seeds

Toss the greens in a large bowl. Set aside.

Brush both sides of the fish with oil and season with salt and pepper to taste. Cook on a lightly oiled grill over hot coals for about 2 minutes per side, or until the fish is firm and opaque. Remove from the grill and keep warm.

Melt the butter in a large sauté pan. Add the vinegar, mirin or sake, and soy sauce and cook over high heat for 1 minute, until slightly thickened. Stir in the scallions and remove from the heat.

Pour all but 2 tablespoons of the warm dressing over the greens and gently toss. Arrange on 2 plates. Top with the fish and spoon the remaining sauce over the fish. Sprinkle with sesame seeds and serve immediately.

SERVES 2

ALMOND-COATED MAHIMAHI WITH MANGO VINAIGRETTE AND GRILLED PLANTAINS

Plantains are a staple of Asian, Latin American, and Caribbean cooking. When they are ripe, the skins are black and the flesh yellow-orange and sweet.

MANGO VINAIGRETTE

2	large ripe mangos, peeled and diced	1	teaspoon lime zest, finely chopped
	Olive oil	½	teaspoon salt
2	tablespoons fresh lime juice	¼	teaspoon freshly ground pepper

½	cup chopped almond slices	2	ripe plantains, skin almost black
¼	cup cracked peppercorns	4	large radicchio leaves
4	mahimahi steaks (about 6 to 8 ounces each and 1 inch thick), split down the center vertically		Parsley or cilantro

In a small bowl, combine the mangos, ¼ cup olive oil, lime juice, zest, salt, and pepper. Chill until ready to use.

Combine the almonds and peppercorns on a sheet of wax paper. Brush the fish with a little oil and season with salt on both sides. Roll the fish in the almond mixture.

Peel and cut the plantains into long diagonal slices, about ¼ inch thick. Brush with oil. Place the fish on an oiled grill over hot coals in the center of the grill and the plantains on the outer edge where it is not as hot. Grill the fish about 5 minutes per side, or just until the fish is firm and opaque and the almonds are deep brown. Grill the plantains 3 to 4 minutes per side, brushing with oil if necessary, until they are scored and soft.

Place a radicchio leaf cup on each plate and spoon in the vinaigrette. Arrange equal portions of fish and plantains on the plates and garnish with parsley or cilantro.

SERVES 4

Almond-Coated Mahimahi with Mango Vinaigrette and Grilled Plantains

SCALLOP SALAD WITH AVOCADO, WHITE CORN, AND MAUI ONIONS

Prawns are also nice with this salad, which was inspired by friend and chef Jeff Vinion. Serve it with Basil Bread (page 136) or a good crusty country loaf.

½ to 1 cup Balsamic-Lime Vinaigrette (recipe follows)

2 ears white corn, kernels scraped and lightly steamed (about 3 minutes)

3 ripe Italian plum (Roma) tomatoes, peeled, seeded, and diced
Salt and freshly ground white pepper

4 thick slices Maui or any other sweet onion (about 1 medium)
Olive oil

16 large sea scallops (about 2 pounds)

12 ounces mixed baby lettuces, cleaned and dried

1 avocado, peeled and sliced

In a small bowl, mix 1 tablespoon Balsamic-Lime Vinaigrette with the corn. In a separate bowl, mix 1 tablespoon vinaigrette with the tomatoes. Season each mixture with salt and pepper to taste. Cover and set aside.

Brush the onion slices with olive oil and season with salt and pepper to taste. Place away from the hottest part of the grill and cook over hot coals for 10 to 15 minutes, or until soft. Set aside and keep warm if necessary.

Brush the scallops with olive oil and grill over hot coals for 3 to 6 minutes, turning frequently and brushing with a little oil as necessary, until just opaque. (Cooking the scallops on a vegetable grilling rack will enable you to turn and remove them easily.) Do not overcook. Remove from the grill and keep warm.

Toss the greens with just enough vinaigrette to coat and place on 4 plates. Arrange the corn and tomatoes in separate piles on one end of each plate. Fan the avocado slices on the other end of each plate. Strew the onion slices and scallops down the center, on top of the greens. Serve immediately.

SERVES 4

BALSAMIC-LIME VINAIGRETTE

½ cup olive oil
⅓ cup balsamic vinegar
    Juice of 1 lime

1 tablespoon sugar
½ shallot, peeled and minced
    Salt and freshly ground pepper

Whisk together all the ingredients. Adjust the seasoning to taste.

MAKES ABOUT 1 CUP

GRILLED SHRIMPS WITH CHIPOTLE-ORANGE SAUCE AND TOMATILLO SALSA

ЭΙΙΙΙΓ

Serve these shrimps as an appetizer course on a hot summer day.

4 limes
1 head butter lettuce, leaves separated
2 ripe avocados
16 large shrimps (about 1 pound), peeled
   and deveined, tails on
   Olive oil

   Salt and freshly ground pepper
1 orange, thinly sliced
   Cilantro sprigs
2 cups Agustine's Tomatillo Salsa Cruda
   (page 151)
½ cup Chipotle-Orange Sauce (page 155)

Juice 3 of the limes. Cut the other lime into thin slices and set aside.

Arrange the lettuce on 4 plates. Peel and dice the avocados and sprinkle with lime juice. Arrange the avocados on top of the lettuce. Set aside.

Brush the shrimps all over with olive oil, season with salt and pepper, and grill over hot coals for 1 to 2 minutes per side, until opaque. Sprinkle some lime juice over the shrimps.

Arrange 4 shrimps around the lettuce on each plate. Garnish with orange and lime slices and cilantro. Serve with Agustine's Tomatillo Salsa Cruda and Chipotle-Orange Sauce on the side.

SERVES 4

LULA BERTRAN'S GRILLED SHRIMPS AND SCALLOPS WITH MANGO MAYONNAISE AND FRIED CILANTRO

Lula Bertran is one of the premier chefs of Mexico, a well-known food writer, and a good friend of Gerri's. It was at one of Lula's cooking classes that Gerri made this recipe. Fried cilantro will stay crisp for several days stored in an airtight plastic bag lined with paper towels. Spinach, parsley, watercress, mint, mustard, and baby beet greens can also be prepared this way.

FRIED CILANTRO

Vegetable oil

4 cups loosely packed cilantro, leaves only, washed, dried, and chilled

---

6 jumbo shrimps, peeled and deveined
6 large sea scallops
Olive oil
Salt and freshly ground pepper

Juice of 2 limes
1 large mango, halved and scored
1 lime, thinly sliced
Mango Mayonnaise (recipe follows)

In a wok, heat 3 cups vegetable oil to 370° F. Deep-fry the cilantro in small batches for 5 to 15 seconds, until the leaves are bright green and almost translucent. Remove with a slotted spoon. Drain on paper towels and keep warm in a low oven.

Lightly brush the shrimps and scallops with olive oil. Season with salt and pepper to taste. On a lightly oiled grill or in a grill basket over medium-hot coals, cook the scallops 1½ to 3 minutes per side, and shrimps for 3 to 4 minutes per side, or just until opaque and lightly marked.

Just before serving, sprinkle the fried cilantro with a little lime juice and salt. Arrange the cilantro, shellfish, and mango on 2 serving plates and garnish with lime slices and Mango Mayonnaise.

SERVES 2   →

Lula Bertran's Grilled Shrimps and Scallops with Mango Mayonnaise and Fried Cilantro

MANGO MAYONNAISE

1 cup packed mango pulp (1 large mango)
1 tablespoon fresh lime juice
½ teaspoon finely grated lime peel
2 teaspoons white wine vinegar

½ teaspoon salt
¼ teaspoon cayenne
¼ cup olive oil

Combine all the ingredients except the oil at high speed in a blender. With the blender still running, add the olive oil drop by drop until the mixture begins to thicken. Continue adding the oil in a very slow, steady stream until all the oil is well incorporated. Adjust the seasonings to taste. Chill until ready to serve.

MAKES ABOUT 1¼ CUPS

LOBSTER WITH FOUR-GRAIN SALAD

This healthful grain salad is easy to prepare. You can vary the combination of grains and greens to your taste or use one cup of any leftover cooked grains of your choice. The lobster can be served warm or cold, or replaced by any shellfish.

2 live lobsters or 2 precooked lobsters (1 to 1½ pounds each)

GRAINS
2 tablespoons wild rice
2 tablespoons brown rice
2 tablespoons barley

2 cups plus 2 tablespoons homemade chicken stock or canned broth
1 teaspoon olive oil
2 tablespoons couscous

VINAIGRETTE
¼ cup Basil Oil (page 160)
2 tablespoons balsamic vinegar

½ teaspoon coarse sea salt
¼ teaspoon freshly ground pepper

Basil Oil, for brushing
¼ cup finely snipped chives
1 tablespoon minced red onion
¼ pound mixed baby greens (about 2 large handfuls or 4½ cups)

Salt and freshly ground pepper
1 Italian plum (Roma) tomato, peeled, seeded, and diced
Finely chopped basil leaves
Whole basil leaves

If using live lobsters, they can be parboiled the day before and refrigerated.

Bring a large pot of water to a rolling boil. Make sure the claws are secured with a rubber band before dropping the lobsters headfirst into the pot. Cover and cook for 2 minutes. Carefully remove the lobsters from the pot with long tongs. (If using precooked lobsters, this step is not necessary.)

When cool enough to handle, place each lobster on its back and separate the head from the body and tail with a large knife. Remove the coral (if a female lobster) and tomalley and reserve for another use or discard. Split the tail down the underside vertically, not cutting completely through.

Twist or cut off the claws. Slightly crack them with the back of a little mallet or a heavy knife handle. Refrigerate the tail and claws until ready to use. Discard the remaining shells and legs or save for stock.

Rinse the wild rice, brown rice, and barley in a strainer under cold water. Place in a medium-size pot and add the chicken stock and oil. Bring to a simmer and cook, covered, over low heat for 35 minutes, or until the grains are chewy and tender. Remove from heat. Lift the cover and stir in the couscous. Cover for 5 minutes. Drain the grains and spread on a tray or platter to cool and dry.

Meanwhile, in a small bowl, whisk together the vinaigrette ingredients and set aside.

Brush the underside of the lobster with a little Basil Oil. Grill the claws on the outer edge of a hot grill, covered, for 10 to 12 minutes, turning several times. Grill the tail over medium-hot heat, flesh side down, about 10 minutes, until the flesh is opaque throughout. When the lobster can be handled, crack the claws with a hammer or nutcracker and remove the flesh in one piece. Remove the meat from the tail in one piece and cut into ½-inch slices.

Meanwhile, scrape the grains into a large bowl. Stir in the chives and onion until well incorporated, then toss with the greens.

Toss the salad with just enough vinaigrette to moisten. Season with salt and pepper to taste and add more vinaigrette if necessary. Arrange the salad in the middle of 2 plates. Top with the lobster and claws, and drizzle them with a little Basil Oil. Sprinkle with some tomato and chopped basil. Garnish with basil leaves and serve.

SERVES 2

TOM MITCHELL'S LIME SHRIMPS WITH BLACK BEAN VINAIGRETTE

Tom Mitchell is a hiking buddy of Gerri's. She ate these shrimps at his house one Sunday afternoon and never forgot them.

6 ounces Corona or any Mexican beer
Juice of **3** limes

¼ cup packed chopped cilantro leaves

¼ cup peeled and diced roasted red peppers

VINAIGRETTE

3 tablespoons sherry wine vinegar

9 tablespoons peanut oil or safflower oil
Salt and freshly ground pepper

⅓ cup cooked or canned black beans, rinsed and drained

SALAD

¼ large jicama, peeled and cut into finger-size sticks (about 1 cup)

1 bunch radishes (about **10 to 12** radishes), trimmed, washed, and sliced

¼ teaspoon salt

2 pounds large shrimp, peeled and de-veined, tails on

2 tablespoons peeled and chopped roasted poblano chile

1 serrano or jalapeño chile, seeded and finely minced

1 tablespoon peeled and chopped roasted red pepper

2 bunches watercress (about **3** cups), thick stems removed, washed and dried

Combine the beer, lime juice, cilantro, peppers, and salt in a medium bowl. Pour over the shrimp and marinate at room temperature for 15 minutes.

Meanwhile, make the vinaigrette. Combine the vinegar, oil, and salt and pepper to taste in a medium bowl. Mix in the beans, chiles, and pepper.

Toss the jicama, radishes, and watercress in a medium bowl and arrange on 4 plates. Pour about 3 tablespoons vinaigrette over each salad. Set aside.

On a lightly oiled grill, cook the shrimps over medium-hot coals, 1 to 3 minutes per side, or until just opaque. Serve immediately with the salad.

SERVES 4

SEA SCALLOPS WITH BELL PEPPER VINAIGRETTE

Large sea scallops, which measure up to about 1½ inches in diameter, are briny and sweet at the same time. Since timing is critical when grilling scallops, it might be easier to put them on a lightly oiled vegetable grilling rack that can be placed on top of the regular grill, then quickly removed as soon as the scallops are done.

BELL PEPPER VINAIGRETTE

- 1 orange bell pepper, stemmed, seeded, white pith removed, and cut into ¼-inch dice
- 1 yellow bell pepper, stemmed, seeded, white pith removed, and cut into ¼-inch dice

- 1 red bell pepper, stemmed, seeded, white pith removed, and cut into ¼-inch dice
- 1½ tablespoons chopped chervil
- ⅓ cup extra-virgin olive oil
- 1½ tablespoons fresh lime juice
  Salt and freshly ground pepper

- 2 pounds large sea scallops
  Olive oil

Salt and freshly ground pepper
Chervil leaves

Combine the peppers and chervil with the oil and lime juice. Season with salt and pepper to taste. (You may need to adjust the amounts of oil and lime juice, depending upon the size of the peppers.) Set aside.

Remove the small membrane from each scallop. Brush the scallops with oil and season with salt and pepper. Cook on a lightly oiled grill over hot coals for 3 to 6 minutes, turning frequently and brushing with a little oil as necessary, just until opaque. Do not overcook. Remove the scallops to a serving platter. Spoon the bell pepper vinaigrette over each scallop. Garnish with chervil leaves. Serve immediately.

SERVES 4

GRILLED SHRIMPS, JACK CHEESE, AND AVOCADO TOSTADA

⊐ I I I I ⊏

Any fresh shellfish, such as scallops, lobster, or crabmeat, can replace the shrimps in this salad.

1 medium head romaine lettuce	2 tablespoons chopped white onion
2 cups Fluffy Avocado-Tomatillo Salsa (page 154)	½ cup chopped cilantro
	8 corn tortillas
½ pound fresh tomatillos, husked, washed, and chopped into ¼-inch dice	2 pounds medium shrimps (about 48), peeled and butterflied, tail on
2 ripe tomatoes, seeded and chopped	Corn or olive oil
½ pound Jack cheese, cut into ¼-inch chunks	Salt and freshly ground pepper
	¾ cup cooked or canned black beans, rinsed and drained
1 large ripe avocado, peeled and diced	Cilantro leaves

Remove and discard the first 3 or 4 dark outer leaves of the lettuce if they are ragged. Wash and dry the lettuce, then slice horizontally into ½-inch strips.

Combine the Fluffy Avocado-Tomatillo Salsa with the diced tomatillos, tomatoes, cheese, avocado, onion, and chopped cilantro. Set aside.

Lightly brush the tortillas and shrimps with oil, and season shrimp with salt and pepper. Over hot coals, grill the tortillas 1½ to 2 minutes per side, until lightly browned, and the shrimps 1 to 1½ minutes per side, until opaque and firm.

To assemble, place 2 tortillas each on 4 plates. Spoon 3 tablespoons black beans on top. Place the lettuce on the beans. Spoon the salsa mixture on top of the lettuce, then top with the shrimps. Garnish with cilantro leaves.

SERVES 4

SEAFOOD SAUSAGES ON CATALAN TOMATO BREAD WITH FAVA BEAN SALAD

Catalonia, situated in northeastern Spain, is famous for its *Pa amb Tomàquet*. Thick slices of country bread are rubbed with tomato, then drizzled with olive oil, topped with sausage or anchovies, and served as a light meal. Try this sandwich version for a summer lunch. Most gourmet markets sell mild and spicy seafood sausages.

2 pounds (about 8) seafood sausages
⅓ cup extra-virgin olive oil
8 thick slices country French or Italian bread
2 garlic cloves, peeled and halved lengthwise

4 very ripe small tomatoes (preferably homegrown), halved
Salt
Fava Bean Salad (recipe follows)

If using sausage that is not precooked, bring a large pot of water to a boil. Randomly pierce each sausage 6 or 7 times with a toothpick and add to the pot. Lower the heat and gently poach the sausages for 10 minutes. Drain. (You can do this ahead of time and refrigerate the sausages until ready to grill.)

Brush the sausages with a little oil and place on a well-oiled grill or griddle over medium-high heat. Brush with oil as necessary during cooking to prevent the sausages from sticking. Grill for about 8 minutes, turning so the sausages are evenly scored and lightly browned on all sides. Set aside and keep warm.

Meanwhile, lightly grill or toast the bread on both sides. Rub both sides of the bread with the garlic, then the tomatoes, gently squeezing as you rub so bits of tomato and juice remain on the surface. Discard the garlic and tomatoes. Drizzle a little of the remaining olive oil on both sides of the bread and then sprinkle the bread with salt to taste.

Place 2 slices of bread on each serving plate, and top with sliced sausage rounds, using 2 sausages per plate. Serve open-faced with Fava Bean Salad.

SERVES 4

→

FAVA BEAN SALAD

Try to buy the smallest fresh beans available. Large ones have a tough outer skin that needs to be removed. If you have to use large beans, it's easiest to pop the bean out of its skin under cold running water after cooking.

2	pounds small unshelled fava beans, or 1 to 1¼ pounds shelled or 2 (10-ounce) packages frozen	2	tablespoons freshly squeezed lemon juice
2	large sprigs cilantro	2	garlic cloves, crushed
¼	cup extra-virgin olive oil	1	medium shallot, minced
			Salt and freshly ground pepper
		¼	cup chopped Italian parsley leaves

Shell the beans. Place the beans and cilantro in a large pot, cover them with water, and bring to a boil. Lower the heat, partially uncover, and cook for 10 to 15 minutes (7 to 10 minutes for frozen), until tender, depending on the size of the beans. Drain, discard the cilantro, and cool at room temperature in a large bowl.

Meanwhile, whisk together the oil, lemon juice, garlic, shallot, and salt and pepper to taste. Let sit about 15 minutes, then remove the garlic. Toss the beans with the vinaigrette. Add the parsley, toss again, and serve at room temperature.

SERVES 4

CALAMARI STEAK AND COLESLAW SANDWICH

Calamari steaks are cut from giant squid that are found in the waters off Mexico and South America. The firm-fleshed, delicately sweet meat is very lean and is similar in taste to abalone. Calamari will be tender if quickly cooked over very high heat.

4	(7-ounce) calamari steaks	4	kaiser, French, or large rolls
⅔	cup good-quality olive oil		Salt and freshly ground black pepper
1¼	teaspoons ground cumin		Helen's Light Coleslaw (recipe follows)
⅛	teaspoon cayenne pepper		

Place the calamari in a Ziploc bag or shallow pan. Mix together the oil, cumin, and cayenne in a measuring cup. Pour ½ cup of the mixture over the calamari, reserving the rest. Turn to coat evenly and marinate in the refrigerator for 1 hour.

When ready to grill, stir the reserved marinade with a fork to redistribute the spices. Split the rolls, then lightly brush the cut sides with the marinade. Grill, oiled side down, about 1 minute, or until lightly toasted. Keep warm. Lift the calamari from the marinade and drain for a few seconds. Season with salt and pepper. Cook on a lightly oiled grill over hot coals 2 minutes per side, or until just opaque, turning once. Do not overcook or the steaks will be tough and rubbery.

Place the calamari on the bottom half of each roll. Top with ½ cup coleslaw. Close the sandwiches and cut in half. Serve with additional coleslaw if you wish.

SERVES 4

HELEN'S LIGHT COLESLAW

My friend Helen Bercovitz, who is a retired caterer, can never provide exact measurements when she gives a recipe. This version of her coleslaw is closest to what she prepared for her clients for many years. If you can find garlic chives, use them instead of the common garden variety. Since the slaw contains no mayonnaise, it travels well to picnics and potlucks. It will keep for 3 to 4 days in the refrigerator.

1 small head green cabbage (about 1¼ pounds), cored and finely sliced	3 scallions, including green tops, thinly sliced
1 red bell pepper, stemmed, seeded, ribs removed, and sliced lengthwise into matchsticks	1 teaspoon chopped chives or garlic chives
	5 tablespoons champagne vinegar
1 green bell pepper, stemmed, seeded, ribs removed, and sliced lengthwise into matchsticks	¼ cup canola or corn oil
	½ teaspoon garlic powder
	Salt and freshly ground pepper

Toss together the cabbage, peppers, scallions, and chives in a large bowl. Mix together the vinegar, oil, and garlic powder and toss with the slaw. Season with salt and pepper to taste. Serve immediately if you prefer crisp cabbage, or let stand 1 hour so the flavors blend and the cabbage wilts.

MAKES 1 CUP

GRILLED SALMON BLT

Who doesn't love a BLT? This version of the sandwich has a delicious and sophisticated twist that is sure to make it a family favorite. Sweet Potato Chips (page 142) are a wonderful accompaniment, or serve the sandwich with regular potato chips, if you prefer.

8 slices thick bacon
4 (6-ounce) salmon fillets
   Olive oil
   Freshly ground pepper
¼ cup Lemon-Chive Mayonnaise
   (page 159)

8 slices of Brioche (page 135) or other
   homemade bread, cut thick
8 medium slices beefsteak tomatoes
1½ ounces assorted baby greens
   (about 2 cups)

Grill the bacon for 3 to 5 minutes, or until crisp, turning once or twice. Drain on a paper towel. Set aside and keep warm.

Brush the salmon fillets with a little oil and sprinkle with pepper. Grill over hot coals 3 to 4 minutes per side, until just opaque and firm but still moist looking.

Spread the mayonnaise on each slice of bread. Arrange the salmon, bacon, tomatoes, and greens on 4 of the slices. Top with the remaining bread. Cut on the diagonal and serve immediately.

SERVES 4

LOBSTER AND MOZZARELLA MELT

Create a repertoire of interesting melts by varying the grilled fish and cheese. Ahi tuna and fontina, halibut and sharp Cheddar, and salmon and dilled Havarti are just a few delicious combinations.

2 tablespoons chopped fresh basil	2 tablespoons Basil Oil (page 160)
2 tablespoons chopped tomato	2 French, kaiser, or any large crusty rolls
Salt and freshly ground pepper	½ avocado, cut into 8 slices
1 whole grilled lobster (page 122)	3 ounces buffalo mozzarella, cut into 6
Aïoli (page 158)	slices

Combine the basil and tomato. Season with salt and pepper to taste. Set aside.

Coarsely chop the lobster meat. Toss with just enough Aïoli (about 3 tablespoons) and Basil Oil to moisten to taste.

Split the rolls and spread each side with a little Aïoli. Layer the bottom halves with the avocado, lobster mixture, and cheese. Place the top halves on a medium-hot grill, cut side down. Grill about 1 minute, or until lightly browned. Remove and keep warm. Place the bottom halves on the grill, cheese side up, away from the hottest part. Close the grill or cover, grilling 3 to 5 minutes, or until the cheese has melted but is not dripping. Top the cheese with the basil-tomato mixture, close the sandwiches, and serve immediately.

SERVES 2

Variation

Replace the Aïoli and Basil Oil with Pesto Mayonnaise (page 159). Mix with the lobster meat. Spread a little Pesto Mayonnaise on each slice of bread and proceed as above.

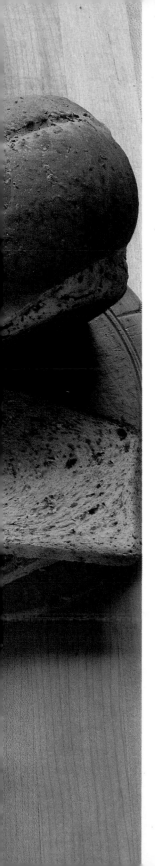

BREADS, SPREADS & SIDE DISHES

BREADS

Brioche

Basil Bread

Chapati

Rosemary-Garlic Focaccia

SPREADS AND SIDE DISHES

Chunky Eggplant Salad

Raita

Potato-Chive Cakes

Black Olive Spread

Sweet Potato Chips

Hummus

Guacamole

A ccompaniments might not always be necessary to a meal, but they complement the main dish, adding another dimension to its taste and appearance.

You'll find that the breads, spreads, and sides offered here will work as well with some of your own favorite dishes as they do with the recipes we've suggested. Since we believe meal preparation should be as easy as possible, if you can purchase a similar product, by all means do. But we also hope you'll be tempted to make some of the recipes that follow. Our version of Basil Bread, for example, is definitely worth taking the time to bake. And the loaves freeze beautifully, so you can always have some on hand.

Spreads such as Hummus and Black Olive Spread will enhance a variety of sandwiches, from a pita stuffed with roast turkey to a quick crostini or bruschetta. And potato lovers will welcome two delicious side dishes—Potato-Chive Cakes and Sweet Potato Chips—both easy to prepare.

PRECEDING SPREAD: *Basil Bread (page 136), Brioche (opposite), and Rosemary-Garlic Focaccia (page 138)*

BRIOCHE

Brioche is traditionally composed of a large round of dough topped by a smaller round. This recipe, which is baked in a loaf pan, slices easily and makes a delicious sandwich bread.

1 tablespoon yeast	1 teaspoon salt
1 tablespoon sugar	6 ounces unsalted butter, very soft, plus
½ cup warm milk	butter for bowl and pan
2¼ cups all-purpose flour	3 large eggs

Dissolve the yeast and sugar in the milk in the bowl of an electric mixer and allow to proof, about 10 minutes. Using the paddle on medium speed, turn the mixer on and add 1 cup flour and the salt. Beat 2 minutes.

Add the butter and beat 2 minutes. Add the eggs, one at a time, beating after each addition. Replace the paddle with the dough hook. Slowly add the remaining flour and knead for 5 minutes, or until the dough is shiny.

Put the dough in a buttered bowl and cover with plastic wrap or a damp cloth. Allow it to rise in a warm place for 2 hours. Punch down the dough, cover with a damp cloth, and refrigerate for about 4 hours, or until the dough is firm enough to be handled.

Place the dough on a floured board and gently form into an oblong shape. This is a very sticky dough, so it's best to handle it as little as possible. Place the dough in a generously buttered 9×5×3-inch loaf pan and let it rise until almost doubled in bulk. The time will vary depending on how warm the kitchen is.

Preheat the oven to 400° F. Bake the loaf for 30 to 35 minutes, until golden brown. The loaf should sound hollow when lightly tapped with your knuckles. If the bread begins to brown too quickly, cover it loosely with some foil.

Let the bread cool a few minutes in the pan before removing to a rack to cool completely. The brioche is best eaten the same day, or it can be frozen.

MAKES 1 LOAF

BASIL BREAD

Gary Chorost, a friend and professional baker, created this wonderful bread. Any herb can replace the dried basil. If your mixer is not large enough to accommodate all the ingredients, knead the dough in two batches or by hand.

6 cups bread flour	½ cup sugar
2 cups dried basil leaves	5 cups water
2 tablespoons yeast	8 cups all-purpose flour
½ pound unsalted butter, cut into pieces	Butter, shortening, or oil for the pans
1 teaspoon salt	

In the large bowl of an electric mixer, combine the flour, basil, yeast, butter, and salt with the paddle attachment at medium speed until the mixture is the texture of coarse meal.

In a large bowl or measuring cup, dissolve the sugar in the water and slowly add to the dry ingredients with the machine still running. Slowly add the all-purpose flour 1 cup at a time. After the fourth cup, remove the paddle and re-place with the dough hook. Keep adding the flour until the dough is no longer sticky. The amount of flour you continue to add will vary depending on the weather and the humidity. Knead with the hook until the dough is pliable, smooth, and elastic, 7 to 10 minutes.

Remove to a large greased bowl and cover with plastic wrap. Put in a warm place to rise for about 45 minutes, until doubled. Punch down and remove to a floured surface.

Preheat the oven to 350°F. Have ready 3 greased 12×5-inch loaf pans.

Cut the dough into 3 equal-size pieces and roll each into a ball. Cover and let rest for 5 minutes, then roll each ball out into a rectangular shape not exceeding the length of the bread pan, about 2½ inches thick. Roll each piece up into a cyl-inder, pinch the ends to close, and place, seam side down, into the pans. Bake for 35 minutes, or until the bread is pale golden and sounds hollow when tapped with your knuckles. Let the bread cool a few minutes in the pan before removing to a rack to cool completely.

MAKES 3 LOAVES

CHAPATI

These large, tortilla-type Indian flat breads are made with *atta,* a fine whole wheat flour sold in Indian and Middle Eastern markets. Finely ground whole wheat flour or whole wheat pastry flour may be substituted.

½ cup *atta*

½ cup all-purpose flour

   Pinch salt

⅔ cup plus 2 tablespoons water

½ cup melted unsalted butter

Sift the flours and salt into the bowl of a food processor fitted with the cutting blade. With the motor running, add ½ cup water and process for 1 minute. Gradually add the remaining water, processing for about 3 minutes.

Remove the dough from the processor. It will be soft. Divide into small walnut-sized pieces. Turn the processor on and drop the balls through the tube one at a time. Process for about 1 minute, until the dough has combined into a large ball.

Transfer the dough to a floured surface. Let rest 10 minutes.

Divide the dough into 10 equal pieces and shape into balls. Flatten and roll them as thin as possible (about 1⁄16 inch thick) into round pancakes, about the same thickness as a tortilla, sprinkling with a little flour as necessary.

Heat an ungreased griddle and cook one chapati at a time. Press with the back of a large spoon to flatten any small blisters that puff up on the surface while cooking. Turn with tongs or a spatula and cook on the other side until golden. Brush with melted butter on one side and roll up in a damp tea towel until ready to serve.

MAKES 10 CHAPATI

ROSEMARY-GARLIC FOCACCIA

This recipe can be halved, or the dough can be frozen, then thawed and baked.

2 teaspoons yeast	6 large garlic cloves, peeled and slivered
2 cups warm water	4 sprigs fresh rosemary, leaves only
5 cups all-purpose flour	2 teaspoons salt
1 teaspoon salt	Freshly ground pepper
Olive oil	

Dissolve the yeast in ¼ cup water in a large mixing bowl. After the yeast activates and is completely dissolved, stir in the remaining water. Stir in the flour and salt. Knead on a lightly floured surface until smooth and elastic, about 10 minutes.

Place the dough in a large, lightly greased bowl. Cover with plastic wrap and let it rise in a warm place until doubled, about 1 to 1½ hours.

Punch down and knead briefly on a lightly floured surface. Replace the dough in the bowl and allow to double again, about 1 hour.

Preheat the oven to 400°F. Generously oil two 9½×13½-inch or 15½×10½-inch baking sheets. Set aside.

Divide the dough in half. On a lightly floured surface, roll out each piece of dough into a 9×12-inch rectangle. Place each piece on an oiled baking sheet.

Pour 2 tablespoons oil over each loaf and gently rub into the top with your hands. Insert thin slivers of garlic over the surface, then sprinkle with rosemary, salt, and pepper to taste. Bake for 20 to 25 minutes, until golden brown. Serve warm, cut into 6 pieces each.

MAKES 2 FLAT LOAVES

CHUNKY EGGPLANT SALAD

The eggplant can be chopped in a blender or food processor, but chopping it in a wooden bowl with a *mezzaluna*, an inexpensive Italian curved chopping tool, gives this salad the best consistency. Serve with pita bread or crackers.

2 medium eggplants (about 3 pounds)
2 tablespoons extra-virgin olive oil
¼ cup seasoned rice vinegar
½ red onion, chopped (about ¼ cup)
4 garlic cloves, minced

1 tablespoon chopped oregano
1 tablespoon chopped chives
¼ teaspoon chili powder
Salt and freshly ground pepper
Cilantro or parsley leaves, for garnish

Pierce eggplants with a fork, then rub with a little oil. Grill over medium-hot coals for about 45 minutes, or until the skins are charred and the insides are very soft, carefully turning several times (see Note). Cool to room temperature.

Peel the eggplants and remove the stems. Chop with a *mezzaluna* until almost smooth and a little chunky. Drain the excess liquid.

Mix the pulp with the remaining ingredients. Adjust seasonings to taste. Transfer to a smaller bowl and cover. Chill at least 30 minutes. Garnish with cilantro leaves before serving. This will keep for 2 to 3 days in the refrigerator.

MAKES 4 CUPS, OR 8 SERVINGS

Note: To cook the eggplants indoors, pierce first, then roast over a medium-high flame directly on the burner, turning to char all sides. Bake on a foil-lined cookie sheet in a 450° F. oven for 45 to 55 minutes, or until soft and collapsed.

RAITA (SPICED YOGURT)

Raitas can be made with any combination of vegetables or fruit added to yogurt. Use hothouse cucumbers in this raita because they don't have to be seeded.

1 hothouse cucumber, peeled and diced
1 tablespoon chopped onion
½ teaspoon salt
¼ cup chopped cilantro

1 teaspoon ground cumin, toasted in a hot skillet for 30 seconds
1 cup plain yogurt

Combine all the ingredients in a small deep bowl. Adjust the salt to taste. Chill at least 1 hour before serving. This is best served the day it is made.

MAKES 2 CUPS

POTATO-CHIVE CAKES

⊐ I I I I ⊏

These delicious and crispy little pancakes can be cooked several hours in advance and rewarmed just before serving.

1 large baking potato	½ teaspoon white pepper
¼ cup grated onion	½ teaspoon salt
¼ cup finely chopped fresh chives	Peanut oil
1 large egg yolk, lightly beaten	

Peel and coarsely grate or shred the potato. Combine with all the remaining ingredients except the peanut oil. Heat 1 tablespoon oil in a large nonstick skillet or on a griddle over medium-high heat. Add 1 heaping tablespoon potato mixture to the skillet or griddle. Flatten slightly and fry 1½ to 3 minutes on each side, or until lightly browned. As you fry the cakes, add additional oil as necessary. Place on paper towels to absorb the oil before serving. Serve immediately.

MAKES 8 TO 10 SMALL CAKES

BLACK OLIVE SPREAD

⊐ I I I I ⊏

For a quick and easy appetizer, make some crostini by spreading the pesto on rounds of grilled Italian or French bread.

½ cup oil-cured black olives, pitted	1 garlic clove, peeled
4 anchovies, washed and patted dry	1 teaspoon grated orange zest
1 tablespoon finely chopped fresh chives	1 cup olive oil
1 tablespoon coarsely chopped fresh rosemary	1 tablespoon fresh lemon juice

Combine the ingredients in a blender or food processor. Process only until the mixture is a coarse puree. It should not be too smooth. Store, covered, in the refrigerator for up to 2 weeks.

MAKES ABOUT ¾ CUP

SWEET POTATO CHIPS

You can use either red yams or the starchier, drier yellow sweet potatoes. These chips are always a big hit, so you might want to double the recipe.

4 medium sweet potatoes or yams, scrubbed	Peanut oil Salt

Slice the potatoes ⅛ to ¹⁄₁₆ inch thick or as thin as possible with a sharp knife, a mandoline, or the slicing blade of a food processor, dropping the slices into a large bowl of ice water as you work. Refrigerate at least 2 hours before frying. Just before frying, drain the potatoes in a colander, then lay the slices flat on a lint-free kitchen towel or on paper towels and pat them completely dry.

Have ready a large roasting pan lined with paper towels. Pour 2 inches of oil in a heavy Dutch oven, chicken fryer, or wok and heat the oil to 375°F. Fry the potatoes in small batches over medium-high heat, maintaining the oil's temperature. As the potatoes crisp and turn brown, 30 seconds to 1 minute, remove them with a slotted spoon to the paper towel–lined roasting pan. Let the oil come back to the required temperature before frying each batch.

Place the roasting pan, uncovered, in a low oven (275°F.), to keep each batch of potatoes warm as it drains. Just before serving, sprinkle with salt to taste. Remove the paper towels and warm in a slow oven (325°F.) before serving. If you're making the potatoes several hours in advance, reheat them on a cookie sheet in a preheated 400°F. oven for about 5 minutes.

SERVES 4 TO 6

Variation: French-Fried Sweet Potatoes

Cut the potatoes into long steak fry–type sticks (about ½ inch thick). Proceed as above, cooking the potatoes until they turn golden brown, are soft, and float to the top of the oil.

PRECEDING SPREAD: *Potato-Chive Cakes (page 140)*

HUMMUS

⊐ ⊓⊓⊏

Hummus is a Middle Eastern dipping sauce made of pureed chick-peas (garbanzo beans). We prefer using canned chick-peas for expediency. Tahini (ground sesame seeds) is available in health food stores and Middle Eastern grocery stores.

1 cup canned chick-peas, drained, liquid reserved
⅓ cup tahini
1 tablespoon coarsely chopped garlic (about 2 cloves)

⅓ cup fresh lemon juice
Salt and freshly ground pepper
Olive oil
½ teaspoon paprika

Combine the chick-peas, tahini, garlic, and lemon juice in a blender. Puree until smooth, adding a little of the chick-pea liquid to thin, if necessary.

Scrape the mixture into a small bowl. Stir in the salt and pepper to taste. Drizzle a little olive oil on top and sprinkle with paprika.

Serve the same day as a dip, or spread on crackers, bagel chips, or pita bread.

MAKES ABOUT 1½ CUPS

GUACAMOLE

⊐ ⊓⊓⊏

Haas avocados from California make the best guacamole because of their buttery texture. If possible, assemble the ingredients at the table, since guacamole is best served as soon as it is made.

4 ripe medium Haas avocados, seeded and peeled
½ white onion, finely chopped

1 garlic clove, finely chopped
1 or 2 jalapeño chiles, seeded
Juice of 1 lime (about 2 tablespoons)

Mash the avocados with a fork until chunky. Stir in the remaining ingredients.

MAKES ABOUT 4 CUPS

CONDIMENTS
&
SAUCES

Grilled Red Pepper Sauce

Apple-Tomatillo Salsa

Red Onion Confit

Tomato and Mint Sambal

Grilled Onion and Garlic Relish

Cranberry Chutney

Agustine's Tomatillo Salsa Cruda

Pico de Gallo

Tomatillo Sauce for Tacos

Chiles in Orange Escabèche

Garam Masala

Fluffy Avocado-Tomatillo Salsa

Chipotle-Orange Sauce

Summer Mango Chutney

Marinated Sun-Dried Tomatoes

Barbecue Sauce

Aïoli

Mayonnaise

Basil Oil

Garlic Oil

Pesto

You're sure to find several recipes in this chapter that will become part of your culinary repertoire. The relishes, chutneys, and sauces are simple to prepare, most taking only a few minutes. The recipes can easily be doubled or tripled. (Many of these recipes use fresh chiles, so before handling them, please see page 36.)

The fresh salsas should be used within a day or two, but the other relishes have quite a long shelf life—the chutneys seem to last forever and get better with age—and they make wonderful gifts.

PRECEDING SPREAD: *Pesto (page 161), Mayonnaise (page 159), and Chipotle-Orange Sauce (page 155)*

GRILLED RED PEPPER SAUCE

This sauce will keep in the refrigerator for 5 days.

2	large red bell peppers	1	teaspoon chopped fresh oregano leaves
4	medium garlic cloves	½	teaspoon ground cumin
¼	cup olive oil	¼	teaspoon cayenne pepper
2	teaspoons lemon juice		Salt and freshly ground pepper

Grill the peppers over very hot coals for 10 to 15 minutes, until blackened. Place in a paper bag and steam for about 15 minutes. Peel off the charred skin with your fingers or a sharp paring knife. Cut the peppers in half and remove the stem and seeds.

Place the peppers and the remaining ingredients in a food processor and process to a thick puree. Cover and refrigerate until ready to serve.

MAKES ABOUT 1¼ CUPS

APPLE-TOMATILLO SALSA

The combination of the tomatillos and green apple lends itself particularly to grilled chicken. Always make sure to wash away any sticky residue left on the tomatillos after removing the husks.

1	pound tomatillos, husked, washed, and quartered	1	serrano chile, deveined and seeded
1	green apple, cored and quartered	½	cup cilantro, leaves only
			Juice of 1 lime

Place all the ingredients in a blender and puree until smooth. Store tightly covered in the refrigerator for up to 1 week. Serve at room temperature or chilled over grilled chicken.

MAKES ABOUT 2 CUPS

Red Onion Confit (opposite), Cranberry Chutney (page 150), and Grilled Onion and Garlic Relish (page 150)

RED ONION CONFIT

This savory marmalade is good hot, warm, or at room temperature. Serve a small amount on the side with any meat or poultry. Store, covered, in the refrigerator up to 1 month.

¼ cup unsalted butter

¼ cup olive oil

2 pounds red onions, sliced

½ cup sugar

Salt and freshly ground pepper

⅓ cup red wine

⅓ cup red wine vinegar

In a large, nonreactive saucepan, heat the butter and oil together. Add the onions, sugar, and salt and pepper to taste. Cook, covered, over moderately low heat for 30 minutes. Add the wine and vinegar and simmer, uncovered, 30 minutes more, or until thick. Store up to 6 weeks in a tightly covered jar in the refrigerator.

SERVES 6 TO 8

TOMATO AND MINT SAMBAL

Very refreshing and low in calories, this is considered a fresh chutney, not to be confused with a cooked fruit chutney. It's a good accompaniment for grilled fish.

4 ripe tomatoes (about 1½ pounds), chopped

2 large sprigs mint, finely chopped (about 2 tablespoons)

1 medium shallot, finely chopped

1 tablespoon fresh lime juice

1 teaspoon salt

1 small jalapeño chile, peeled, seeded, and diced (optional)

¼ teaspoon coarsely ground pepper

Combine all the ingredients in a bowl. Refrigerate until ready to serve. Store tightly covered in the refrigerator for up to 2 days.

MAKES 3 CUPS

GRILLED ONION AND GARLIC RELISH

⅃ I I I I ⊏

Serve this relish with any grilled meat or poultry. The flavor improves if the relish is made several days before serving. Serve hot or at room temperature, or store in the refrigerator for up to 1 week. Vary the onions or use one kind.

1	large red onion	2	tablespoons red wine vinegar
1	large white or yellow onion	1	tablespoon fresh whole thyme leaves
1	large sweet onion (such as Maui, Vidalia, or other preferred variety)	2	teaspoons fresh oregano or marjoram
3 to 4	tablespoons olive oil	2	large whole bay leaves
5	garlic cloves, peeled and thinly sliced	¼	teaspoon red chile flakes, or to taste
1	tablespoon sugar	¼	teaspoon salt
			Freshly ground pepper

Peel and thickly slice the onions. Brush both sides with a little olive oil. Grill over hot coals, turning as necessary, about 5 minutes, or until almost tender and lightly browned on both sides. Watch that the onions don't get too soft.

Heat the remaining oil over high heat in a large skillet. Add the onions and garlic and cook, stirring, for 3 minutes, until the onions are slightly tender. Sprinkle with sugar, stir, then add the vinegar, thyme, oregano or marjoram, bay leaves, and chile flakes. Cook an additional 1 or 2 minutes, just until the vinegar evaporates. Season with salt and pepper to taste.

MAKES ABOUT 3 CUPS

CRANBERRY CHUTNEY

⅃ I I I I ⊏

This recipe looks far more complicated than it is. The mélange of flavors produces a unique spicy-sweet relish that goes well with any grilled poultry. The recipe can be easily doubled. Stored in tightly covered containers in the refrigerator, the chutney will keep for up to 6 months.

12 ounces cranberries, fresh or frozen	1 tablespoon honey
1 small onion, finely chopped	1 garlic clove, minced
¼ cup water	1 large cinnamon stick
7 tablespoons red wine vinegar or apple cider vinegar	1 tablespoon finely chopped fresh ginger
1 small orange, unpeeled, seeded, and coarsely chopped	¼ teaspoon crushed red chile seeds
	¼ teaspoon ground cinnamon
½ cup mixed dried fruit or golden raisins	¼ teaspoon ground cloves
½ cup granulated sugar	¼ teaspoon ground nutmeg
3 tablespoons dark brown sugar	¼ teaspoon cayenne

Combine the cranberries, onion, water, and vinegar in a medium stainless steel pot. (If using frozen cranberries, it is not necessary to thaw them first.) Bring the ingredients to a boil and cook about 5 minutes, or until the cranberries are soft. Lower the heat and add the remaining ingredients. Simmer, uncovered, stirring occasionally, until the mixture thickens, about 30 to 45 minutes.

Remove the cinnamon stick and cool before serving.

MAKES 2½ TO 3 CUPS

AGUSTINE'S TOMATILLO SALSA CRUDA

Agustine Marcial, one of the cooks at Gilliland's, created this recipe, a perfect partner to fresh tomato salsa. It will keep for 2 days in the refrigerator.

8 to 10 fresh tomatillos, peeled, washed, and quartered	½ large white onion, cut into small wedges
2 large garlic cloves, peeled	1 or 2 jalapeño chiles, seeded and deveined
2 cups cilantro, leaves only	Salt and freshly ground pepper

Place all the ingredients except the salt and pepper in the bowl of a food processor or blender. Process until almost pureed. Add a little water if necessary to blend. Season with salt and pepper to taste. Serve at room temperature.

MAKES ABOUT 2 CUPS

PICO DE GALLO

⊐ I I I I ⊏

This spicy, chunky salsa is one of the most commonly used in Mexican and South-western cooking. It's a necessary accompaniment to fajitas, but it's also delicious with any grilled food or as a flavoring for meat loaves, mixed salads, omelets, and even tuna salad. If you can't find serrano chiles, jalapeños make a milder substitute. The recipe can be easily doubled and will keep, covered, in the refrigerator for 2 days.

4 or 5 large ripe tomatoes, seeded and coarsely chopped
1 medium red or white onion, finely chopped
1 to 2 small serrano chiles, seeded and minced

1 garlic clove, minced
1 cup fresh cilantro leaves, chopped (reserve several whole leaves for garnish)
Juice of **1** lime
Salt to taste

Combine all the ingredients in a nonreactive bowl. Garnish with cilantro leaves. Serve at room temperature.

MAKES 3 TO 4 CUPS

TOMATILLO SAUCE FOR TACOS

⊐ I I I I ⊏

This cooked tomatillo sauce will keep in the refrigerator for at least one week. If you can't find fresh tomatillos, you may substitute canned.

1 pound fresh tomatillos, husked and washed
2 cups cilantro leaves, chopped

4 jalapeño chiles or **2** serrano chiles, seeded and deveined
½ cup finely chopped white onion
2 teaspoons salt

Boil the tomatillos in lightly salted water for 5 to 7 minutes, or until soft. (Omit this step if using canned tomatillos, but rinse them off.) Drain, reserving the liquid. Puree the tomatillos in a food processor or blender. Add the remaining ingredients and process just until combined. If necessary, thin with a little tomatillo water. Cool slightly before stirring. This salsa can also be served warm, at room temperature, or cold. Store, covered, in the refrigerator for 2 days.

MAKES 2 CUPS

CHILES IN ORANGE ESCABÈCHE

This is another recipe inspired by Lula Bertran. Escabèche is a method of pickling cooked foods, especially fish and chicken, in a spicy cold vinegar marinade that originated in Spain. The escabèche marinade itself can be used as a basting sauce for any grilled meats or as a salad dressing. Remember to wear gloves when seeding the chiles. The chiles taste better after several days in the marinade. Store in the refrigerator for 3 to 4 weeks.

2 cups water	½ teaspoon ground allspice
½ cup apple cider vinegar	½ teaspoon fresh thyme leaves
6 small ancho chiles of equal size, tops removed, seeded	½ teaspoon fresh marjoram leaves
	½ teaspoon salt
10 garlic cloves, peeled	¼ cup orange juice
1 large onion, sliced	½ cup olive oil

Boil the water with ¼ cup vinegar. Remove from the heat and add the chiles. Let sit for 30 minutes.

Meanwhile, in a medium, nonreactive shallow pan, combine the remaining ¼ cup vinegar with the remaining marinade ingredients. Remove the chiles from the water, drain, and place in the marinade. Cover and store in the refrigerator at least 24 hours before using.

SERVES 6

GARAM MASALA
(INDIAN GROUND SPICE MIXTURE)

There are many variations of this toasted spice mixture from northern India. It can be purchased in Indian and gourmet markets, but fresh is best and it's easily made. Like all spices, it should be stored in an airtight container in a dark, dry, cool place and replaced with a fresh batch every 6 months.

5 (3-inch) cinnamon sticks	**¼** cup coriander seeds
½ cup whole cloves	**¼** cup black peppercorns
½ cup cumin seeds	

Preheat the oven to 200°F.

Spread the spices in one layer on a large cookie sheet and roast for 30 minutes, stirring several times. Do not allow to brown.

Cool to room temperature, then pulverize in a blender at high speed until finely ground.

MAKES 1 CUP

FLUFFY AVOCADO-TOMATILLO SALSA

This pale green salsa is fantastic on poached salmon. Tomatillos are available in many produce stores and most Latin American markets throughout the country. Do not substitute canned tomatillos for fresh. The sauce will keep for up to 2 days in the refrigerator, but it is best used the day it is made.

10 medium tomatillos, husked and washed	**2** tablespoons peanut oil
½ small white onion, peeled	Salt and freshly ground pepper
1 garlic clove, peeled	**1** large ripe avocado
1 jalapeño chile	**1** tablespoon red wine vinegar
2 cups water	**1** tablespoon extra-virgin olive oil
1 cup cilantro leaves, tightly packed	**1** teaspoon fresh lime juice

Place the tomatillos, onion, garlic, and jalapeño in a medium saucepan. Cover with the water. Cook over medium heat for 15 to 20 minutes, or until the tomatillos are soft but not mushy. Drain the vegetables, reserving the water. Place the warm vegetables and the cilantro in a blender. Puree, adding just enough cooking liquid to make a thick puree.

Heat the oil in a medium sauté pan and add the puree. Cook over medium-low heat about 5 minutes to thicken and blend the flavors. Season to taste with salt and pepper. Cool to room temperature. Pour into the blender, add the avocado, and puree until the avocado is well incorporated. Blend in the vinegar, olive oil, and lime juice. Serve chilled.

MAKES 2 CUPS

CHIPOTLE-ORANGE SAUCE

Gerri based this sauce on a recipe created by her friend Martha Chapa, a famed painter and food writer in Mexico. Chipotles are dried and smoked jalapeño chiles that can be purchased pickled or in adobo, a vinegary tomato sauce. Both can be purchased in Mexican markets.

¼ cup peanut oil	1 teaspoon sugar
1 pound tomatillos, peeled, washed, and chopped	Juice of 3 oranges
2 chipotle chiles in adobo, chopped	1 teaspoon ground cumin
	Salt

Heat the oil in a saucepan over medium-high heat. Add the tomatillos and chiles and cook several minutes, or just until soft. Add the remaining ingredients. Gently simmer over medium heat, 20 to 25 minutes, until the sauce has thickened and reduced to about 2 cups. Cool and serve at room temperature within 24 hours.

MAKES ABOUT 2 CUPS

SUMMER MANGO CHUTNEY

You can use a combination of green papayas and mangoes for an equally delicious chutney. It will keep indefinitely in the refrigerator.

2	medium onions, peeled		3	cups light brown sugar, firmly packed
2 or 3	jalapeño chiles, seeded		2	cups red wine vinegar
4	ounces fresh ginger, peeled and cut into 1-inch pieces		1	tablespoon ground cinnamon
3	garlic cloves, peeled		1½	teaspoons salt
1	medium lime, unpeeled, seeded, and cut into wedges		1	teaspoon ground cloves
5	ripe but firm mangoes, peeled and cubed (about 5 to 6 cups)		1	teaspoon ground allspice
			½	teaspoon cayenne
			½	tablespoon black mustard seeds
			½	tablespoon ground cumin

Coarsely chop the onions, jalapeños, ginger, garlic, and lime in a food processor. Do not overprocess.

Place the mixture in a large stainless steel saucepan, bring to a boil over high heat, and add the remaining ingredients. Lower the heat and simmer, uncovered, 1 to 1½ hours, stirring frequently, until the fruit is tender.

Let cool, then pour into 2 tightly covered 1-quart containers and refrigerate.

MAKES ABOUT 2 QUARTS

Variation: Pumpkin or Banana Squash Chutney

Replace the mangoes with 5 cups peeled and cubed pumpkin or banana squash, and proceed as above.

MARINATED SUN-DRIED TOMATOES

Rehydrated sun-dried tomatoes taste even better marinated in flavored oils, and best of all, the oil itself can be used. Store in the refrigerator up to 6 months.

3 cups water
6 ounces sun-dried tomatoes
8 garlic cloves, peeled
2 sprigs fresh rosemary

2 sprigs fresh oregano or marjoram
1 teaspoon black peppercorns (optional)
   Extra-virgin olive oil

Boil the water in a medium saucepan. Add the tomatoes and simmer for 2 minutes. Drain immediately and layer the tomatoes between 2 double thicknesses of paper towels, changing the paper several times, until the tomatoes are dry. (It is sometimes easier to blanch and dry them in 2 batches.)

Layer the tomatoes, garlic, rosemary, oregano, and peppercorns if using in a 2- to 3-cup jar with a tight lid. Pour enough olive oil in the jar to reach the top and completely cover the tomatoes. Cover the jar and let sit overnight in the refrigerator. Before using, bring to room temperature, then blot the tomatoes with paper towels to remove excess oil.

MAKES ABOUT 2 CUPS

BARBECUE SAUCE

This sauce can be easily doubled and will keep for 2 months in the refrigerator.

2 cups smoked barbecue sauce
3 tablespoons molasses
¼ small onion, diced
¼ red bell pepper, diced

¼ cup chopped mixed fresh herbs, such as
   basil, thyme, and parsley
1 tablespoon Worcestershire sauce
1 teaspoon prepared Dijon mustard

Mix all the ingredients in a large bowl. Cover and chill until ready to use.

MAKES 3 CUPS

AÏOLI

Aïoli is a very garlicky mayonnaise-type sauce from Provence that is delicious with grilled chicken or fish. It is traditionally made without eggs and prepared in a mortar. For convenience, this aïoli can be made in a blender or food processor.

6 to 8	medium garlic cloves	2	large egg yolks, at room temperature
½	teaspoon kosher salt	1	cup mild virgin olive oil

Place the garlic, salt, and yolks in a blender or food processor. With the blender on high speed or while the processor is running, slowly add the oil in a very thin stream until it is absorbed and an emulsion is formed. Adjust salt to taste. Serve immediately or cover and refrigerate until ready to use.

MAKES 1 TO 1¼ CUPS

Variation: Roasted Garlic Aïoli

Replace the raw garlic with 12 to 14 cloves unpeeled garlic that have been roasted in a little oil in a 350°F. oven for ½ hour. Peel the garlic and proceed as above.

Variation: Apple Aïoli

Peel, core, seed, and cube 1 large green apple. Cook with 2 tablespoons water in a small pot just until soft and still chunky, about 5 minutes. Drain the apples if there is too much liquid. Prepare the aïoli as above, blending in the apple, but omit the eggs and reduce the oil by half. Serve as an accompaniment with pork.

MAYONNAISE

There is absolutely no comparison between jarred and fresh mayonnaise. The secret to making perfect mayonnaise is to add the oil very slowly so the emulsion does not break. For a lighter flavor, use canola or any mild-flavored oil.

1 large egg, at room temperature
1 tablespoon fresh lemon juice
¼ teaspoon kosher salt

¼ teaspoon white pepper
1 cup olive oil

Place all the ingredients except the oil in a blender and blend on high speed until incorporated. With the blender running, add the olive oil drop by drop until the mixture begins to thicken. Continue adding the oil in a very slow, steady stream until an emulsion forms and all the oil is absorbed. Serve immediately or cover and refrigerate until ready to use.

MAKES ABOUT 1 CUP

Variation: Lemon-Chive Mayonnaise

Stir ½ tablespoon grated lemon zest and 2 tablespoons finely chopped chives into the prepared mayonnaise.

Variation: Pesto Mayonnaise

Add ¼ cup Pesto (page 161) to the ingredients in the blender jar before adding the oil. Proceed with recipe as above.

BASIL OIL

The oil will last several months in the refrigerator. You may replenish the basil and oil as you use the contents of the jar.

½ cup coarsely shredded basil leaves   Extra-virgin olive oil
1 garlic clove, peeled

Place the basil and garlic in a dry 2-cup jar or container. Fill to the top with oil and cover. Store in the refrigerator. Before using, bring to room temperature.

MAKES ABOUT 2 CUPS

GARLIC OIL

Since olive oil congeals when it is chilled, this oil, when spread cold on bread, makes a flavorful as well as healthy alternative to butter.

2 garlic bulbs   Olive oil

Peel the garlic cloves. Place them in a 2-cup jar and fill to the top with oil. Let the oil stand a few hours or overnight at room temperature before using. As the oil is used, it can be replaced. Store unused oil in the refrigerator, but bring it to room temperature before using.

MAKES ABOUT 1¾ CUPS

PESTO

Pesto is truly a taste of Italy, having originated in Genoa, where it is customarily served on pasta. This emerald green sauce is also wonderful as a flavoring for soups, as a garnish for grilled meat, chicken, or fish, and even as a topping for a baked potato. For a quick antipasto, spread a little pesto on slices of Italian bread and run them under the broiler just until the pesto is bubbly.

2 cups fresh basil leaves, tightly packed	¼ cup freshly grated Parmesan cheese
4 garlic cloves	½ cup extra-virgin olive oil
½ cup pine nuts	

Put the basil, garlic, and pine nuts in a food processor and process to a thick puree. Add the cheese and pulse several times to blend. Slowly add enough oil to make a thick paste. Transfer to a jar or plastic container with a lid if not using immediately. Cover with a thin layer of olive oil and store in the refrigerator for several weeks or freeze for several months.

MAKES 1 CUP

Variation

Pesto made with dill or cilantro instead of basil makes an excellent topping for fish or chicken, or a sauce for pasta.

For the above recipe, use 2 cups of either fresh dill leaves or cilantro leaves. If you're using cilantro, reduce the pine nuts to ¼ cup. If you're using dill, add 1 teaspoon sugar.

GLOSSARY

COMMON AND UNCOMMON GREENS

Gourmet and natural foods shops and most large supermarket chains offer a diverse selection of greens, from ordinary lettuces to organic and restaurant-quality produce. Some markets offer prewashed baby greens sold loose, or in five-ounce or larger packs, that usually contain ten to twelve kinds of greens and herbs. Variety lettuces, grown in baskets to be snipped when desired like herbs, are also available in many stores. Ethnic and farmers' markets are wonderful places to discover new and exotic varieties of greens.

ARUGULA was a favorite green of the ancient Romans and is still popular in Mediterranean cuisine. Sold in bunches with the roots attached, the deeply lobed emerald to gray-green leaves have a delicate peppery flavor and should be eaten when very young. The pale lavender flowers are also edible. (Also called rocket, rocket cress, roquette, rugula.)

BEET GREENS or tops, are the dark green, red-veined leaves of the beet, with an earthy, grasslike flavor. The yellow leaves of golden beets have a similar taste.

BELGIAN ENDIVE is produced by planting the root of the witloof chicory plant underground in moist soil. The result is a five- to six-inch-long compact head—resembling a squat oval cigar—with slightly bitter, cream-colored leaves. (Also called endive, French endive, witloof chicory in Britain.)

BOK CHOY, a staple in Oriental cooking, consists of about ten to fourteen smooth, white-veined, celerylike stalks eight to ten inches long. The crisp stalks have a mild, sweet lettuce flavor, the raw dark green leaves a spicier, cabbagelike taste. Hearts are also sold, topped with yellow flowers. (Also called Chinese chard cabbage, Chinese mustard cabbage, Chinese white cabbage, lei-choi, pak choi, Japanese white celery mustard, taisin.) **Baby bok choy** has slightly crisp and crunchy pale green stalks with a mild sweet flavor. The raw leaves are slightly sharp. Grill the whole plant to bring out the sweetness. (Also called mei qing choy, Shanghai bok choy, green bok choy, ts'ing kang bok choy.)

BROCCOLI RABE, a favorite Italian vegetable, has long, crisp, succulent ribs, ragged leaves, and tiny clusters of broccolilike flower buds with a lively, mildly pungent, almost horseradishlike flavor. Canola oil (rapeseed) is made from the seeds. (Also called broccoli raab, rapini, broccoletti di rape, ruvo kale, yu choy, cime di rapa.)

CABBAGE is grown commercially in several hundred varieties, the most common of which are the strong-flavored green and red cabbages with round, compact heads and smooth, waxy leaves. Broccoli, brussels sprouts, cauliflower, and kale are also part of the cabbage family.

CHICORY, radicchio, endive, and escarole are all related. **Curly endive,** sometimes called chicory in the United States, is a strong, bitter green, with narrow, frilly dark green dandelionlike leaves that fade into pale green interior leaves. In the United States, the softly textured young chicory is usually referred to as *frisée.* The spiked leaves of the blanched ivory and pale green varieties add volume to any salad. (Also called *chicorée frisée,* curly leaf endive.)

CHINESE CABBAGE is a nearly cylindrical head resembling a pale green football. The crinkly, crisp leaves, which graduate in color from white at the bottom to pale green at the top, are similar in texture to romaine lettuce and celery and have a sweet, mild flavor. Another variety, **long Napa cabbage,** is about twice as long, with more slender leaves and a stronger flavor. You can use both kinds of the cabbage as you would lettuce, or try it shredded for slaw, pickled, steamed, or stir-fried. (Also called Chinese celery cabbage, Chinese leaf, chou de Chine, bow sun, hakusai, Michihili, Napa, Peking cabbage, petsai, Shantung cabbage, siew choy, Tientsin cabbage, wong bok.)

CHOY SUM has medium-size tender pale green stalks that resemble the interior stalks of bok choy. The oval green leaves and the flower buds can be used as well. (Also called Chinese Tsai shim, flowering white cabbage, mock pak choi.)

CHRYSANTHEMUM GREENS, although native to the Mediterranean, are extremely popular in Asian cuisine. A member of the mustard family, these aromatic greens have an unusual, strong flavor. Use the young leaves, stems, and flowers like spinach in salads, or in stir-fries or sukiyaki. (Also called chop suey greens, garland chrysanthemum, tong ho, shungiku.)

COLLARDS, a staple of southern cooking, are a variety of kale. The large, heavy green leaves and the stems have a slightly bitter flavor similar to both cabbage and kale. (Also called collard, collard greens.)

CRESS is hot and peppery. The variety known as **pepper, curled, mountain,** or **garden cress** has fine leaves. Another variety, called **upland, winter,** or **yellow rocket cress** (a member of the mustard family) has dark green broad leaves. Both grow on dry land. **Watercress** (a member of the nasturtium family) grows wild in and along shallow, freshwater streams. The small smooth, round leaves grow on a tender, crunchy stalk. (Also called creasy greens.)

DANDELIONS appear on the market in very early spring. The leaves of cultivated plants are longer, wider, and more tender than those of wild dandelions. The young, tangy, slightly bitter notched leaves are best raw in salads. Older greens are traditionally wilted or braised in the South. They are very rich in iron and vitamin A.

ESCAROLE is a broad-leaf variety of endive. The large, bitter, slightly pungent green leaves have a tangy mustardy flavor that complements hearty bean salads. Green Curled Ruffec has frilly, ragged leaves; Full Heart Batavia, has crisp, lettucelike leaves that are curled and closely bunched. (Also called flat or broad chicory, Batavian endive in Britain.)

FENNEL, used throughout the Mediterranean, has a delicate, nutty aniselike taste. The feathery, pale green filigreed leaves of **sweet fennel** are used as an herb or a garnish; both the celerylike stalks and flattened bulbous base of *finocchio* are delicious sliced raw into salads, grilled, or braised. (Also called Florence fennel.)

FIDDLEHEAD FERNS, the tightly coiled, tiny fronds of any new fern growth, have an earthy asparagus–green beanlike taste, and are a good source of vitamins A and C. They grow in damp forested areas, mostly in the eastern United States. Buy only bright green shoots no more than 1½ inches in diameter and use them as soon as possible. (Also called ostrich fern.)

FRISÉE (See chicory.)

GAI LOHN is similar to broccoli rabe. Cultivated for its thick, flowering stems and small leaves and flower buds, this Chinese native is usually harvested young, before the sharp, slightly mustardy flavor becomes too strong. (Also called Chinese broccoli, Chinese kale, white flowering broccoli, gai laan.)

KALE is beautiful as well as nutritious. A favorite in the South, it tastes like a cross between broccoli and cabbage. The curly leaves vary from blue-gray to green-purple. (Also called seen choy, sien ts'ai, borecole, curly kale, colewort.)

LEAF AMARANTH is usually sold in small bunches and used like spinach. The young, rounded leaves vary in color from green and yellow to deep red and have a distinctive, bittersweet flavor. (Also called Chinese spinach, hin choy, hsien shu, hiyu, lal sag, cholai bhaji.)

LETTUCE is available in more than 100 different varieties that fall into the following categories:

   ICEBERG (HEAD) lettuce—firm, round well-folded heads with crisp pale green leaves; the best-selling lettuce in the United States. (Also called crisphead, cabbagehead.)

   BUTTERHEAD (BOSTON)—loosely folded green or reddish-green outer leaves and sweet cream-colored inner leaves, with a delicate buttery flavor. The **limestone** (Bibb) variety is smaller with mild-flavored, dark green, crisp but tender leaves. Other varieties include large **buttercrunch** and European baby **marvel** (Merveille de Quatre Saisons), with beautiful burgundy- and pink-edged leaves.

   ROMAINE (COS)—clusters of tall, upright, extremely crisp leaves. Discard the dark green outer leaves and use the greenish white interior leaves. Baby romaine and hearts of romaine are the most delectable, having a sweet, nutty flavor. They can be found in specialty stores. Romaine traditionally is used in Caesar salad. Varieties include ballon, bronze, green, Paris white, and red.

   LEAF lettuce—fragile, single leaves on stems forming thick bunches. The outer leaves can be frilled and crumpled, or deeply lobed, varying in color from light green to red and brownish red. Flavor ranges from mild to slightly bitter. **Lollo rossa** has rose-colored or red-brown tips and blistered and frilly leaves. Other varieties are Black Seeded Simpson, bronze leaf or prizehead, lollo bianco, red and green oak leaf, and salad bowl.

LEEKS, which are sweet and mild, can be used just like scallions when immature. They're delicious eaten whole, raw or grilled.

MÂCHE has a sweet, nutty flavor and is popular in Europe as a summer salad ingredient. The spoon-shaped green leaves are delicate and quite perishable, which accounts for its high price, so they should be used right away. (Also called corn salad, fetticus, field salad, lamb's lettuce, lamb's tongue, rapunzel.)

MALABAR SPINACH is an unusual mild Asian green with thick, flat, bright green oval leaves and stems. The leaves also can replace okra as a thickener for soups and stews. (Also called basella, Indian spinach.)

MINER'S LETTUCE is a tart wild herb with pale green, tender, spoon-shaped leaves. The stems are also edible, and the flowers have a pleasant and slightly buttery flavor. (Also called winter purslane, Montia perfoliata.)

MITSUBA, which grows wild in Japan, is a tall, sweet parsley with flat, heart-shaped light or dark green leaves that grow three to a stalk. Use the seedlings like cress and the young leaves chopped in salads. (Also known as Japanese parsley, Japanese wild chervil, three-leaf celery.)

MIZUNA is closely related to leafy turnips and has been grown in Japan since antiquity. Its thin white stalks bear long, dark green jagged-cut leaves that are mild, with a faint lemon-pepper flavor. (Also called Japanese greens.)

MUSTARD GREENS are the sharpest and most peppery of all hot greens. Before using them, it is advisable to taste them first, since the bite varies from one variety to another. The bright emerald green, large ruffled leaves are a southern favorite, steamed, sautéed, or cooked in broth.

MUSTARDS (ORIENTAL) are pungent and sharp-flavored leaves that can be salted, pickled, or used in salads. The huge wide curled ribs and dark green leaves of the mature **broad-leaf** (dai sum gai choy, ogarashi, or Swatow mustard cabbage) are used for their mild mustard tang. The curled, rounded leaves of **Chinese leaf mustard** (Indian Mustard, bamboo mustard cabbage, gai choy, Green in Snow mustard, serifon) add a not-too-strong, pungent mustardy flavor to salads and sandwiches. **Osaka** (Southern curled mustard) is a pungent purple mustard used in salads when the leaves are young and mild. **Namfong** (Chinese mustard cabbage) is a strong summer variety with thin, tender leaves. In Cantonese cooking, it is often parboiled, then stir-fried with garlic and black beans.

NASTURTIUM adds a wonderful peppery-radish flavor to any salad. Both the golden, red, or orange flowers and dark green rounded leaves are edible. (Also called Indian cress.)

NEW ZEALAND SPINACH has spreading branches and small, arrow-shaped, succulent leaves that can be used interchangeably with spinach.

ORACH is a mild and sweet spinach substitute with two- to three-inch green, yellow, or red leaves. (Also called French spinach, mountain spinach.)

PERILLA is commonly used in Japanese cuisine with sushi and sashimi as both garnish and vegetable. The young leaves and seedlings of both the green (shiso) and red (beefsteak plant) varieties have a unique flavor (the red are richer and spicier than the green) that complements strong-flavored greens. (Also called gee so, tia to.)

PURSLANE, often considered a weed in the United States, has succulent, sharp-flavored oval leaves. They're used raw in salads in France and cooked in meat dishes in Mexico. (Also called verdolago, Carti-choy, summer purslane.)

RADICCHIO is only one of the many varieties of red leaf Italian chicory, of which the two most common are *Rossa di*

Verona, a small, grapefruit-size head with large, loose, and fleshy white and burgundy leaves, and *radicchio di Treviso,* which has crunchy, long, and slender deep red variegated leaves with white ribs. Treviso, a nonheading variety, is particularly delicious grilled. The flavor of both varies from slightly bitter to sharp.

SALAD SAVOY is a flashy ornamental but edible kale. The ruffled and mild-flavored leaves are variegated, ranging in color from white to red or purple tinged with green edges. (Also called flowering kale.)

SCALLIONS can be immature onions, young leeks, or even young shallots. Both the dark green tops and white base are used. (Also called green onions, spring onions, salad onions.)

SORREL has a lemony, grasslike flavor that enlivens such fish as salmon. Use the bright green leaves also in salads, soups, and sauces. (Also called French sorrel.)

SPINACH, which is slightly bitter, can be bought loose, in bunches, or precleaned in 10-ounce packages, ready for the salad bowl. It is a good source of vitamins A and C as well as iron.

SPROUTS are the seedlings still attached to the seeds. The mild-flavored tiny alfalfa and crunchy long white mung bean (so good in Oriental stir-fries) are the most common. Sharper-flavored sprouts can be grown from chia, onions, cress, and radish seeds. Nutty-flavored sprouts include lentil, pea, clover, soybean, and sunflower.

STEM LETTUCE, grown mainly for its stem, comes from China. The crunchy stalks of the mature plant can be used like celery hearts, the leaves like lettuce. (Also called asparagus lettuce, celtus, Chinese lettuce, woh sun.)

SWISS CHARD, a member of the beet family, has large dark green leaves on tall silvery-white flat stalks. Chard is interchangeable with spinach, but it doesn't cook down as much and has a slightly earthier flavor. The thick midrib, which tastes similar to celery, should be removed from the leaf before cooking. **Red Swiss chard** (rhubarb chard), a red-stemmed, red-veined variety, has a stronger flavor, and can sometimes be stringy and tough.

TATSOI is a Japanese flat cabbage that grows in a rosette form. The deep green, spoon-shaped leaves are smooth, firm, and tender. Baby tatsoi is commonly used in gourmet and Asian salad mixes. (It is also called rosette pak choi, or flat cabbage.)

TURNIP TOPS have long green oval leaves with small green or pale yellow flowers and taste similar to mild but bitter mustard greens. Use sparingly if using them raw.

COMMON FLAVORING HERBS

Herbs are the fragrant leaves of flowering plants that do not have a woody stem. Use the whole leaves in salads as you would any other green. Unless otherwise specified, all the herbs called for in the recipes in this book are used fresh.

ANISE grows on tall spindly stalks topped with feathery leaves and tiny yellow flowers that are licorice flavored.

BASIL, or sweet basil, is native to India and akin to mint. The broad, oval leaves and white flowers are slightly spicy and peppery with a suggestion of anise and cloves. This herb is an indispensable flavoring for tomatoes, salads, and sauces, especially pesto, in Italian and Mediterranean cooking. Varieties include anise, bush, cinnamon, Italian, lemon, opal (deep purple leaves), spicy globe, lettuce-leaved, tulsi or sacred, purple ruffles, Thai, Mexican spice, and Genovese. (Also called herbe royale.)

BORAGE is a bushy, cucumber-flavored plant with gray-green, hairy, oval leaves and small blue, starlike, sweet flowers. Add the chopped young leaves to salads. The flowers can be candied.

CHERVIL has delicate, lacy, pale green leaves with a subtle anise-parsley flavor. More popular in France than in the United States, it is an essential ingredient in mesclun. Fines herbes is a mix of chervil, tarragon, chives, and parsley.

CHIVES are perennial members of the onion family. The long, thin, grasslike hollow shoots have a very delicate onion flavor. The lavender or blue blossoms are also edible. **Oriental garlic chives** have flat, broad-leafed shoots with a mild garlic flavor.

CILANTRO has been used since 5000 B.C. The pungent bright green segmented leaves resemble Italian parsley and have a sagelike flavor enhanced with citrus. It is an integral part of Mexican, Asian, Indian, and Caribbean cuisines. The seed, called coriander, is a popular flavoring for cakes, sauces, and soups. (Also called coriander, Chinese parsley, Mexican parsley.)

DILL, one of the most ancient herbs, looks just like fennel. The feathery, blue-green leaves have a mild anise flavor that blends well with fish, especially salmon, and meats. Use also in soups, salads, and in pickling.

EPAZOTE grows wild across the United States. The strong, pungent green leaves are commonly used in Mexican cooking. (Also called Mexican tea, wormseed.)

LEMON BALM has oval, lemon-scented leaves with a trace of mint.

LOVAGE has giant, hollow celerylike stalks that grow three to six feet high and taste like strong, peppery celery. Use the young, glossy, dark green leaves in soups, salads, and stews.

MARJORAM, or sweet marjoram, called "the herb of grace" by Shakespeare, is interchangeable with oregano. The pale gray-green leaves have a delicate and spicy flavor.

MINT is an aromatic, pungent herb with a multitude of medicinal and culinary uses. The cool-flavored, toothed leaves grow on square stems. The taste ranges from fruity to perfumy. Varieties include bergamot, chocolate, corsican, lavender, spearmint, peppermint, apple, pineapple, lemon, pennyroyal, and scotch.

OREGANO is similar to but sharper flavored than sweet marjoram. The small, dark green, toothed aromatic leaves are used extensively in Italian, Spanish, and Mexican cooking to flavor tomatoes, pizza, salads, sauces, and stews. (Also called wild marjoram.)

PARSLEY, unfortunately, is probably used more as a garnish in the United States than for cooking. Of the more than thirty varieties of this slightly peppery herb, the apple green **curly-leaf** variety is most common. **Flat-leaf Italian parsley** has sturdy, more flavorful deep green leaves. Both the leaves and roots are used.

ROSEMARY, native to the Mediterranean, is an aromatic evergreen and a member of the mint family. The pungent, yet sweet, needle-shaped leaves are thick and leathery with a lemon-pine aroma. Use both the leaves and flowers.

SAGE, once associated with immortality, is pungent with undertones of lemon, mint, and camphor. The most common variety has silvery gray-green oval leaves and blue flowers. Other varieties include golden, pineapple, purple, and tricolor.

SALAD BURNET has toothed and rounded cucumber-flavored leaves that can be substituted for borage.

SAVORY is related to mint. **Summer savory,** which is more popular, is mild and sweet with a peppery, thymelike flavor. **Winter savory** is stronger with a more pinelike essence. Both have small, oblong dark green leaves that grow on a fuzzy stem. (Also called bean herb.)

TARRAGON is a strong aromatic perennial with dark green spear-shaped leaves. It should be used sparingly. First used by the Arabs, it was brought to Europe from Russia and Asia.

THYME was used by the ancient Greeks as a fumigant, an antiseptic, and an aphrodisiac. The tiny, oblong, fragrant leaves have a mild green taste. Use thyme in salads and to season dressings, poultry, meats, fish, soups, stews, and sauces. Other varieties include golden lemon, creeping, and silver.

SOURCE DIRECTORY

⊐ⅠⅠⅠⅠⅭ

Contact the following companies for information regarding a local distributor or mail order information.

OUTDOOR GRILLS

ARKLA
1600 Jones Road
Paragould, AR 72450
800-356-3612; 501-236-8731
Gas grills.

BELSON PORTA-GRILLS
P.O. Box 207
North Aurora, IL 60542-0207
800-323-5664; 708-897-8489
Party size, gas, charcoal, and mesquite grills.

BROILMASTER
Division of Martin Industries
4200 St. Clair Avenue
Washington Park, IL 62203
618-271-1272
Gas grills.

CHAR-BROIL
W.C. Bradley Enterprises
P.O. Box 1240
Columbus, GA 31993-2499
800-352-4111
Charcoal, gas and electric grills, and accessories.

CHARMGLOW
500 S. Madison Street
Duquoin, IL 62832
618-542-4781
Gas grills, smokers, and accessories.

DUCANE
The Ducane Company
800 Dutch Square Boulevard
Columbia, SC 29210
803-798-1600
Gas grills.

GOURMET GRID
Porcelain Metals Corporation
1400 S. 13th Street
Louisville, KY 40210-1834
502-635-7421
Portable outdoor charcoal grill and accessories.

HASTY BAKE
7656 E. 46th Street
Tulsa, OK 74145
800-4AN-OVEN
Gourmet charcoal ovens in various sizes, natural lump charcoal, wood chips, firestarters, and accessories.

I FORNETTI OVENS
Renato Specialty Products, Inc.
11350 Pagemill Road
Dallas, TX 75243
214-349-5296
Italian woodburning grills and ovens for kitchens and outdoors.

J & R MANUFACTURING
820 W. Kearney Street
Suite B
Mesquite, Texas 75149
800-527-4831; 214-285-4855
Custom home and commercial woodburning grills, smokers, and open barbecue pits.

THE KINGSFORD PRODUCTS COMPANY
1221 Broadway
Oakland, CA 94612
800-232-4745; 415-271-7000
Oval kettle grill and charcoal.

PYROMID PORTABLE OUTDOOR COOKING SYSTEMS
3292 S. Highway 97
Redmond, OR 97756
800-824-4288
Charcoal grills and environmental accessories for kettle grills.

SMOKEY BAYOU OUTDOOR COOKER
P.O. Box 1322
Hammond, LA 70404
504-345-1016
Charcoal and gas oven/grills.

SUNBEAM
4101 Howard Bush Drive
Neosho, MO 64850
800-641-4500; 417-451-4550
Gas and electric grills and accessories.

THERMOS COMPANY
1555 Illinois Route 75 East
Freeport, IL 61032
815-232-2111
Gas grills, tabletop gas grills, accessories, and universal replacement parts.

WEBER GRILLS
Customer Service Center
560 South Hicks Road
Palatine, IL 60067-6971
800-446-1071; 708-705-8660
Gas and charcoal kettle grills, tools, and accessories.

INDOOR GRILLS

BURTON STOVE TOP GRILL
Max Burton Enterprises
502 Puyallup Avenue
Tacoma, WA 98421
800-272-8603

CONTEMPRA
651 New Hampshire Avenue
Lakewood, NJ 08701
908-363-9400
Electric grill.

EL ASADOR STOVE-TOP GRILL
Armer Products Company
P.O. Box 6773
Modesto, CA 95355
209-523-6332
Stovetop hot-air grill.

HOT ROCK
Frieling USA, Inc.
1812 Center Park Drive
Building A
Charlotte, NC 28217-2900
800-827-2582

JENN-AIR
3035 N. Shadeland
Indianapolis, IN 46226
317-545-2271
Built-in gas and electric grills.

LE CREUSET OF AMERICA
P.O. Box 575
Yemassee, SC 29945
803-589-6211
Reversible cast-iron grill/griddle.

MAVERICK INDUSTRIES, INC.
265 Raritan Center Parkway
Edison, NJ 08837
800-526-0954; 908-417-9666
Electric grills and electronic digital thermometers.

T-FAL USA
208 Passaic Avenue
Fairfield, NJ 07004
201-575-1060

THERMADOR
5119 District Boulevard
Los Angeles, CA 90040
800-735-4328; 213-562-1133
Built-in gas grills and griddles.

VICTOR GRILLPAN
Chantry
P.O. Box 3039
Clearwater, FL 34630-8039
813-446-1960
Cast-iron ridged grill pan.

ACCESSORIES AND TOOLS

BAR-B-Q PIZZA BAKER
Salday Products Corporation
P.O. Box 2027
Rockville, MD 20852
301-330-9012

CHARCOAL COMPANION
7955 Edgewater Drive
Oakland, CA 94621
800-521-0505
Chimneys, tools, racks, and grilling herbs.

COOKSHACK, INC.
2304 N. Ash Street
Ponca City, OK 74601
800-423-0698; 405-765-3669
Smokers, preseasoned hardwoods, spice rubs, and sauces.

GRIFFO GRILL
1400 North 30th Street
Quincy, IL 62301
800-486-0700; 217-222-0700
A wide assortment of accessories including baskets, racks, skewers, chimneys, corncob firestarters, and a grill-top wok.

GRILL PARTS DISTRIBUTORS
6150 49th Street North
St. Petersburg, FL 33709
800-447-4557
800-282-4513 (Florida only)
A mail order service specializing in supplying gas grill parts for every gas grill manufacturer.

JACKES-EVANS MANUFACTURING CO.
4427 Geraldine Avenue
St. Louis, MO 63115
800-325-6173; 314-385-4132
Racks, tools, chimneys, grill covers, and universal parts.

FUEL

CONNECTICUT CHARCOAL COMPANY
Old Time Charcoal
61 Wilton Road
Westport, CT 06880
203-227-2101
Hardwood charcoal.

LAZZARI FUEL COMPANY
P.O. Box 34051
San Francisco, CA 94134
415-467-2970
Mesquite charcoal and assorted wood chips.

LUHR JENSEN & SONS
P.O. Box 297
Hood River, OR 97031
503-386-3811
Apple, alder, cherry, and hickory chips.

MAIL-ORDER CATALOGS FOR GRILLS AND ACCESSORIES

THE CHEF'S CATALOG
3215 Commercial Avenue
Northbrook, IL 60062-1900
800-338-3232

COMMUNITY KITCHENS
P.O. Box 2311
Baton Rouge, LA 70821-2311
800-535-9901

COMPANION PRODUCTS, INC.
P.O. Box 59066
Dallas, TX 75299-0066
800-426-3632; 214-241-0107
Accessories for Sunbeam Gas Grills and other tools.

GAZIN'S
Cajun/Creole Gourmet Catalog
2910 Toulouse Street
P.O. Box 19221
New Orleans, LA 70179
800-262-6410

OUTDOOR CHEF
O.D.C., Inc.
P.O. Box 6255
Evansville, IN 47719-0255
800-544-5362
Replacement parts for Arkla grills, universal parts, and accessories.

SUR LA TABLE
84 Pine Street
Seattle, WA 98101
800-243-0852

TEXAS BBQ SPECIALITIES
P.O. Box 1473
Hurst, TX 76053
800-23-Grill

WILLIAMS-SONOMA—A CATALOG FOR COOKS
P.O. Box 7456
San Francisco, CA 94120-7456
800-541-2233

THE WOODEN SPOON
P.O. Box 931
Clinton, CT 06413
800-431-2207

ZABAR'S
2245 Broadway
New York, NY 10024
212-496-1234

GREENS, HERBS & PRODUCE

Most of the following companies sell wholesale as well as retail and have overnight delivery. A minimum order is usually required for fresh produce.

BABY GREENS, EXOTIC VEGETABLES, AND FRESH HERBS

FINES HERBES
16 Leonard Street
New York, NY 10013
800-231-9022

FOX HILL FARM
440 West Michigan Avenue
P.O. Box 9
Parma, MI 49269
517-531-3179

FRESH AND WILD, INC.
P.O. Box 2981
Vancouver, WA 98668
800-222-5578; 206-254-8130

FRIEDA'S, INC.
P.O. Box 58488
Los Angeles, CA 90058
800-421-9477; 213-627-2981

KENTER CANYON FARMS
13402 Wyandotte Street
North Hollywood, CA 91605
818-765-0550

KONA KAI FARMS
1824 Fifth Street
Berkeley, CA 94710
510-486-0289

MALIBU GREENS
P.O. Box 6286
Malibu, CA 90624
800-383-1414

DRIED HERBS

THE HERBFARM
32804 Issaquah-Fall City Road
Fall City, WA 98024
800-866-HERB; 206-784-2222
Dried ten-inch herb bunches.

THE SPICE HUNTER INC
254 Granada Drive
San Luis Obispo, CA 93401
805-544-4466
Grilling herbs.

ITALIAN SEEDS

FRATELLI INGEGNOLI
Corso Buenos Aires, 54
20124 Milano, ITALY
(011) 392-29513167
(011) 392-221420—fax
This company publishes a catalog in English, as well as a huge catalog in Italian with a vast assortment of seeds that are unavailable in the United States. Some American seeds are also sold, so read the catalog carefully to make sure you're not ordering something that can be bought here. Inquiries and orders can be conducted in English with no problem, and paid for with American dollars.

ORIENTAL GREENS, SEEDS, POTTED HERBS, AND DRIED SPICES

NICHOLS HERBS AND RARE SEEDS
Nichols Garden Nursery
1190 North Pacific Highway
Albany, OR 97321
503-928-9280

PREPACKAGED SALAD MIXES

SOLVIVA
Box 582 RFD
Vineyard Haven, MA 02568
508-693-3341

SHIITAKE MUSHROOMS

DELFTREE FARM
P.O. Box 460
Pownal, VT 05261
800-243-3742

INDEX